PREACHER'S
KID

PREACHER'S
KID

TONY BUNTS

ARPress

ILLUMINATING IDEAS
EMPOWERING VOICES

ARPress
45 Dan Road Suite 5
Canton MA 02021

Hotline: 1(800) 220-7660
Fax: 1(855) 752-6001

Ordering Information:
Quantity sales. Special discounts are available on quantity purchases by corporations, associations, and others. For details, contact the publisher at the address above.

Printed in the United States of America.

ISBN-13:	Softcover	979-8-89389-993-1
	Hardcover	979-8-89389-994-8
	eBook	979-8-89389-992-4

Library of Congress Control Number: 2024918660

Being a member of a preacher's family brings on a myriad of expectations. The preacher's wife must always project an image of being in tune with godliness. That is a learned condition where she walks around with an angelic smile and speaks softly to the congregants and is always available with a sympathetic ear and assurances that she will bring up their concerns to the pastor.

The preacher's progeny is expected by everyone to be an example that all people can point to as a kid that the congregants can hold up to their normal children to aspire to. This is not only the expectation of the congregants but also of the preacher. Their mother, who did not get the calling, is responsible to see that they live up to their expectations as the preacher is too busy counseling the congregants and their children.

It is expected of a preacher's kid, that they attend and lead in children and youth groups and that they by example extend the Christian teachings of their father. Also, is expected that a preacher's kid is not worldly. He or she does not really know what life is all about for those who must struggle in the real world to survive. He or she have never been subjected to the words that get a mule team moving on a cold morning or the vagrancies of a Jersey cow who will only quit kicking at the milk bucket when she is told loudly that she is about to receive a swift kick in the ass with proper invectives. They don't really know what life is all about and therefore are really not viable functioning people like normal kids are.

Of course, there is the other expectation of the maverick preacher's kid. He is the kid that gets in trouble just like any normal kid and because he or she does not participate in the ministries to the church is considered a bad seed and unfortunately hinder the ministry of the preacher to his congregants.

CHAPTER 1

My father graduated high school with a driving desire to get into the movie business. He had cousins that were in the business and they helped him get a position within MGM's school of directing in 1935 it was a working school and he learned hands on as well as worked for MGM in many different venues to pay for his room and board.

He was attending church at the St Thomas the Apostle Church (A High Episcopal Church) when he got the call to serve God. Both of his parent's families emigrated from Prussia at different times and were engaged in the evangelical movement that was influenced by Methodism, so he had decided that he would become a Methodist Preacher.

He moved back to El Paso and drove a taxi while he waited for the fall semester to begin. I am going to diverse a minute from the foundational history to tell you about a lesson I learned from my father's experience as a taxi driver. The only place you were able to get fares was at the railroad station. One evening a well-dressed man hopped into his taxi and gave him an address. When they arrived there the man told my father that he needed to go up to a room and that he would like him to come along as a witness and he would give my father a five-dollar bill for his trouble. Five dollars was an enormous sum for such a small chore during the depression and my father agreed. They went up to the room and the man opened the door with a key and they walked in on a man and women in bed, who were obviously scared as was my father. The man walked over to the man's side of the bed, reached in his back pocket pulled out his wallet and said, "When you are through with her give her this dollar bill. That's the way she

1

is going to be getting her money from now on." He then asked my father to take him back to the train station. I know this was a diversion from the story line, but it happened to be one of the best lessons I ever heard from my father as the man chose to settle the dilemma in a final non-violent way.

In the fall of 1937, he headed off to McMurry College in Abilene, Texas. At the same time a very intelligent young lady at the age of 15 years old is Brownfield, Texas for McMurry College. My father played football for the War Hawks and the young lady who would become my mother was cheering him on. They both graduated in the spring of 1941 and culminated their plans to marry in El Paso, Texas before my father started seminary at the Perkins School of Theology on the campus of Southern Methodist University in Dallas, Texas. Mom and Dad moved into a frat house where they were the house parents even though my mom was 19 years old. I was born in Dallas, Texas in 1943, my mother was 21, and my father who was 25 years old was finishing up his bachelor's in divinity and was already doing circuit preaching on the road. I have no clue if I was attending any of those services or not. I know that my father and the fraternity boys were already fitting me out for a football career.

In June 1945, my first younger sibling was born. He was underweight and feeble and required a lot of my mother's attention. Thus began my independent individualism that was to dominate my childhood. I was left to my own devices as my mother was busy with my brother and my father was riding a circuit. I began to explore my world. I don't even intend to imply that I remember those first three years, but by the fourth year, I was beginning to build solo adventures and memories.

October 14, 1945, my father was transferred to Highland Park Methodist Church in El Paso. The church was perched on the foothills of the Franklin Mountains under the east end of scenic drive. The congregation was lower middle class and this is the first time that I would become acquainted with the concept of gangs. Our neighborhood was non-Hispanic and the gangs were created to keep it so. The parsonage was across the street from the church and consisted of two bedrooms and a bathroom. You had to climb two tiers of stairs to get to it as it was backed into the mountain with a slope in the front. As I stated, I was left to my own devices most of the time. We had an ice box anicemd every couple of days the iceman would show up and hoist a block of ice on a pad on his ample shoulder with ice hooks and carry it up to place it in the icebox to keep our food and the milk that the milkman left in front of the door cool. I had my goal for life; I wanted to be a big strong iceman. One of the great disappointments of my life was the acquisition of a refrigerator, but I soon focused on the goal of being a trash man that rode hanging on the back of the truck and swung the contents of those big trash cans in the truck.

Being momma's helper, I already had daily chores. Some of which were: taking out the trash to those cans; using a pestle and mortar to grind a big yellow pill into a powder so that it could be mixed with a block of white vegetable grease so that we could have fake butter (margarine). I refused to eat the stuff and was not introduced to butter until I married a farm girl. Our neighbors to the back had laying hens and they were often traveling, and it became my chore to gather the eggs. It was one of the most terrorizing experiences for a four- and five-year-old to look into the malevolent eye of a chicken with a hard beak and reach in under her to take the eggs that she was sitting.

It was at this time that I had my first revulsion with church. My mother would see that I was all decked out for church and I showed up with ample black curly hair. The women of the congregation would comment to my mother about my beautiful hair and teenage girls would run their hands through my hair and marvel at the natural curls. My pleas to my mom to let me stay home or cut off all my hair fell on deft ears.

My mother's younger sister was a beautiful blond girl whom at the age of 15 ½ married a young man who was a short 20 years old. It was the summer of 1947 when my mother, brother and I boarded a Pullman car and headed out to Long Beach, California to pick up my Aunt who was her husband after nine years of marriage. She had a daughter who was a year older than I and a son who was a year younger, and they would be coming with us. I was 4 ½ years old and my memory is somewhat sketchy, but I do remember my brother throwing a fit as he wanted to sleep on the upper bunk. Mother finally relented and during the night he came plummeting down past my lower bunk and hit the floor. As he had wet the bed, there was no amount of persuasion that would make me take the upper bunk and he had to sleep on the floor. I remember swimming in the ocean and taking my first ride on a wooden roller coaster called the Cyclone Racer. After that, I don't think I ever passed up the chance to ride a roller coaster.

I can't really peg down the time, but it wasn't that much earlier than our trip out to California, that my father bought a 10-year-old car. Up till then we were taking the bus. I know Dad must have had one earlier on, but I have no memory of it, but a 1937 4 door Cord was very impressive, and I felt like a Prince riding in it. Unfortunately, it was not very reliable and in the southwest it tended to vapor lock at the most inopportune time. When my father came out to Long Beach, he was driving his parents 1941 Plymouth and pulling a trailer to pick up us along with my aunt and cousins for the trip back to El Paso. My aunt and cousins lived with us and my aunt was engaged in modeling.

Nothing is ever rose pedals and parades. I had a great affinity toward dogs and really wanted one for myself. As was normal for me, I was awake real early in the morning, when I spotted a German Sheppard walking straight down the street. He was stumbling around, had foam coming out of his mouth and was growling. I really did not approach him, but I did later mention him to my mom. That bought me a series of injections with a long needle in the stomach. It wasn't six months later when both my brother and I were exposed to another dog and we got to have those shots all over again. I still don't like long needles.

It was Christmas time 1947, when we all loaded up and went to Brownfield, Texas to visit our grandparents and show off my new baby sister of whom I had the distinct honor of wheeling her and my mom out of Southwest General Hospital in a wheelchair.

While we were there, a soldier kept appearing at the house and my aunt and he would leave. We returned to El Paso and in April the soldier showed up and my aunt and cousins moved back to Brownfield. It was just a short time later that I was informed that my new uncle was a member of the new United States Air Force and he was a pilot.

For the next 15 years, I would see my aunt's pictures on a billboard looking down at me with a cigarette in her hands and Lucky Strike emblazoned above her head.

CHAPTER 2

It was May 1948, when my father was assigned to the Methodist Church in Fabens, Texas. Fabens is only 31 miles away from El Paso, but at the time it was all of a hour's trip by car and a total change in life's experiences. Fabens was a small town that supported all of the farms that surrounded it. It was the beginning of a rural life's experiences.

The parsonage sat on the northwest corner of the block and the Church was on the southwest corner. Down on the northeast corner sat the home of a Hispanic family who were in the trucking business and they had a son by the name of Bennie. Bennie was the first friend I ever had. My mother never really worried about me as she knew, I was with Bennie. It seemed that Bennie's mother and grandmother always had a pot of beans on the stove. There was also, a flat iron with handmade tortillas cooking on it.

The parsonage was a one-bedroom house with a screened in back porch. My brother and I slept on the porch and our baby sister slept in the bedroom with our parents. The first summer there was idyllic. Bennie and I lived the life of Tom Sawyer and Huckleberry Finn. The King family who were members of the church, consisted of Mrs. King and her two daughters (Betty and Phyllis). Mother had a readymade babysitter in Betty who was a senior in high school. Often that summer, Betty would show up to watch my brother and sister and Mom would gather Bennie and I for an adventure. Most of our adventures consisted of a swim with mom in the town pool, a picnic in the park and an afternoon Matinee. One of my favorite past times was running and mom was always ready for the challenge. We even took out the trash together and raced to the house.

Bennie had learned the art of cat fishing on the Rio Grande which ran between Mexico and the United States. For Bennie and me it was an easy jaunt down to the river. We would head off to the river with our cane poles to fish the holes that Bennie had learned about. There was a lot of cane growing in the areas that the river would rise into when it was running full, and I learned that it was preferable to cut yourself a new pole every time you went fishing so that it would dry and you would have a new pole for the next fishing trip.

The roof on the church had a good overhang and underneath it wasps would build their paper nests. Bennie and I had our cane poles which could reach under the overhang and knock off the nests. We would knock off a couple of nests and beat a retreat, only to come back in a bit and gather up the nests, which were full of larva which were a great temptation for big old catfish to rise out of their hole and scoop them into their mouth along with our hook.

Going to the river usually started with the swim. Bennie and I had confiscated a long piece of hip rope from one of the cattle trailers. We had a great place to fish so we had established a swimming hole about 50 feet down the river from our fishing hole. We shinnied up a cottonwood tree and tied a rope on a limb extended over the river. Usually, the first order of the day was to go swimming. If you got too far out from the bank you would get into the current and we quickly learned that we could not fight the current and we would swim with it and across it until we reach land. It was great fun to grab the rope we had over the river let go. On occasion we would wear ourselves swimming and when we got to the fishing hole we would prop the end of the cane pole against our butt and drift off to sleep waiting for old catfish.

On one of our trips, which were very often, we stopped at Mrs. King's house, which was about a block from the river for a drink of water. Instead, we scored tea and a slice of lemon meringue pie. I left her my catfish and Bennie took his home, so his abuela could cook us some fish to go with the tortillas and beans. It wasn't long before we were thirsty going and coming and there always was some tea and lemon meringue pie.

It was in the early fall, when I came home from Bennie's house to find my mother and father fighting. Dad was very upset that a preacher's wife would expose herself in a swimming suit like a common trollop. Mom was

7

crying and then my father slapped her. He held both her arms and was shaking her when I hit a home run with a soft ball bat on his back. He let go of her and took off his belt and started hitting me when mom grabbed the bat and told him to stop or by God she would kill him. He left the house and from that day on, I never got to go swimming with my mother again. I had learned a lesson. We, as part of the preacher's family, must always live up to the expectations of the congregants for the sake of my father's career. My father and mother would get into arguments and as my father got louder. I would show up with a baseball bat. To my knowledge he never put his hands on my mother again.

It was around that same time that I experienced my first bully. There was a seven-year-old boy on our block that kept trying to fight me and I would run away or do anything I could to avoid fighting a boy that was a head taller than I. On one of the occasions of me running pell-mell into the house to avoid a drudging, my father was there. He felt that I was showing coward and forced me outside to face him. I was getting the worse of it when I had the opportunity to give him a swift kick in the crotch, which ended the fight and put the aggressor to bawling. My father was very irate that I did not fight a fair fight. My mother spoke up and said in her quite southern accent, "J.R. you told him to stand up for himself. What I just observed is that he did a very good job of it." My father walked away very disappointed in me, but not willing to confront mother's logic.

Betty was working at the local print shop and I got into the habit of stopping by to see if I could pick up some work so that I could go to the Saturday afternoon matinees, which most often featured one of our cowboy heroes. As President Truman was running against Thomas Dewey, there were always posters being printed for someone and they needed to be distributed or posted. I made out like a bandit. The printing process was a Linotype and after the letters had been arranged and the sheets were run the slugs would be cleaned in white gas and milted to be reused. On one occasion I was offered a quarter to go down to a local filling station and get a can full of white gas (naphtha). On the way back, some of it slopped out on my leg and gave me quite a burn.

I started school in the fall of 1949. My mother was pregnant again and I was well aware that meant another baby. Bennie and I went to school the first day and before the day was out we had to defend ourselves. The problem is that the principle did not care why we were fighting. The fact that we were fighting earned us 5 swats with a well polished paddle that had holes drilled in it. I was introduced to a policy that my father instituted, and that was if I got paddled at school, I would get a double amount of them at home. This edict came from the same father that had forced me to fight earlier in the year. You can see where I really had a conflict with the irony. Bennies father and brothers took a different tact. Out came some boxing gloves and we were coached on defending ourselves. They felt if we beat up enough boys, we would no longer be going to the principal's office for fighting. They were right on the money and Bennie and I were not above helping each other out if the occasion presented itself.

It was December of 1949 when my mother and father came home from El Paso with a new baby brother. There was a new single bed crowded on to the screened porch, which now had wooden shutters to keep out the cold in the winter. Our two-year-old sister joined my brother and me in wrapping ourselves with cotton blankets against the cold.

Every day in class, whenever the teacher told us to pull out a piece of paper, we were instructed to write our name at the top of the page and write the date. I will never forget the first day of class in 1950, when I got to write the date. I marveled at the idea that the century was halfway through and wondered if it would be any way possible that I would ever be able to see the beginning of another century fifty years from now. I talked with my mother about it and she said we would both do that together. She missed it by nearly a year, but she was in my heart when January 1, 2000 rolled around. I loved her so.

More and more so, I was being enlisted into the functions of the church. I was enlisted to use a push broom in the sanctuary on Saturday or wash the stained glass windows. There was an African Methodist Episcopal Church in Fabens that catered to the black Methodists. They were going to have a big revival week, where they had a service every night. For some reason at the last moment the evangelist, who was to conduct the services couldn't make it and the congregation was in dire straits. They came to my father and asked him if he would consider conducting the revival. He agreed and drug me along. It was one of the best church experiences of my life. The only white people in the church were me and my father and I was asked to be an usher and pass the plate. I have always loved music and the hymns were sung from the heart with gusto. There was so much joy in the congregation. While my father was preaching, there was constant chatter in affirmation of what he was saying, and it was to a beat. My father began to preach to the beat and the voices agreeing with what he was saying, and the constant "Amen Brother". It was Friday evening, and the last sermon was preached when a very large woman came up to my father and gave him a hug and uttered the fatal words that I repeated often to him the rest of his life. They were "Reverend Bunts, you skin is white but you heart is pure Black."

If you drove north from Fabens on a sandy unimproved rut road, you would come to a series of mud cliffs that stuck out into what I have become to believe is the north boundary of the Rio Grande Flood Plain. They stuck out fingers of decaying cliffs southward into the valley. My father saw this as a great opportunity to have an ecumenical sunrise service venue. He had joined every service club that would have him and he pitched it to them as a way to serve the community. He also approached other denominations about having the service. I don't know how that went, but I do know, most of the time it was he and I that started the ball rolling by placing three crosses on three fingers of cliffs. He had somehow obtained some power poles and we spent many a day out on the cliffs notching them to fit together and then bolting them. We dug holes to drop them in and we had help with erecting them and cementing them in. There was one finger that was somewhat longer and it was close to the road that climbed up the cliffs. The three crosses were erected to face the end of that finger where a cement lectern was formed. On Easter, the worshipers would be sitting on chairs in front of the lectern, when the sun would rise behind their backs. I know we had a couple of services there before we moved on.

Fabens High School had no athletic programs and as there were some big strapping farm boys, my father thought there should be a Fabens football team. He got the Lions club to agree to purchase equipment and he got a farmer to bring in a tractor and a piece of equipment to level the ground between the parsonage and the church for a practice field. I bring this up because I got to ride around standing on the hitch in the back of the tractor while he was dragging the most egregious bumps out of existence. It was one of my education points when as we passed over a spot the big tires began to sink and we broke through the top of an ole cesspool. I had not before been acquainted with that phase of plumbing, but I was up to my neck in education.

My father was the coach. Bennie and I were the water boys and what I would later learn to be termed managers. We would collect the pads after practice and stored them for the next day and the players would take their uniforms home to be cleaned by their mother for the next day. I have no clue how many games we played, but I do know that the surrounding towns that had teams were outclassed. When we moved on, the school board elected to take over the Wild Cats as the high school football team.

My relationship with my brother was not good. He was five years old and had no responsibilities. He was still considered feeble, and my parents made him my responsibility and whenever he messed up, I was punished. Neither Bennie nor I wanted him along and on one occasion we bet him that he couldn't ride a truck tire around. Bennie's father had a truck idling and he wrapped himself around one of the trailer tires and hung on. Just as his father was about to pull away one of the neighbors saw him wrapped around the tire and stopped Bennie's father from moving. Of course, I got another paddling because I wasn't watching him. I thought it would be best if I did not argue the point, but both Bennie and I had a good vantage point.

It was a spring Sunday in 1951, and all of us were getting ready for church. My sister had her bath and it was time to brush her hair. It was always a hard time when my mother started getting all of the snags out of her hair. On this morning my sister had enough and went out the front door stark naked. She had gained the street and was running right down in front of the church where the parishioners were arriving. She could run like a gazelle with her blond hair blowing in the wind. Dad was none too happy.

We often saw the Saturday afternoon matinees which were mostly our western heroes. Roy Rogers and Dale Evens came to a premiere showing of one of their shows at the Plaza Theater and the next morning boarded a train east. The train passed through Fabens and we were all marched down to the railroad tracks from school to wave at them as they were on the back platform of the passenger train.

It was late winter of our second year in Fabens when King came into our lives. King, was a collie dog. I was in heaven. I knew my father would not want to feed King so I got the dog food. King became Bennie's and my constant companion for the next couple of months. One day I came home from school and King was gone. My father had given him to a rancher. I did not speak to my father for two months.

CHAPTER 3

My father went off to the Annual Conference and Bishop Smith said you're being assigned to the church in Fort Sumner, NM. As we couldn't afford a moving van, Dad had a trailer hitch put on the back of his car and we barrowed a cotton trailer from one of the farmers in Fabens. Some men helped us and we loaded it with our household goods, put a tarp on it and Dad and I took off for Fort Sumner. We left early in the morning with canvas water bags hanging in front of the radiator, so that we could cool of the motor as we went. It took all day for us to get to Fort Sumner and we finished unloading the trailer the next morning. That was my first time seeing Alamogordo, Ruidoso and Roswell, which for the next six years would become familiar sights as was the Sacramento Mountains. Dad's top speed was about 45 miles per hour and the accent to Ruidoso was even slower with multiple stops to cool of the engine. Once we reached the top at Ruidoso it was even slower because there were no trailer breaks and dad kept the engine in first gear on all of the declines.

It took all day for us to get to Fort Sumner and we finished unloading the trailer. Dad took off for Fabens early in the morning and left me with our household goods and a promise that he would be back by tomorrow evening. I was eight and a half years old.

The house was a palace compared to the homes in El Paso and Fabens. It had a basement and a second story which was a large room that was built three quarter size. There were three bedrooms on the main floor with a kitchen, dining room and a large living room that was dominated on one end with a large fireplace. In the back of the house there was a screened-in porch that extended the length of the house and a large back yard with a barn like structure midway.

Some of the church ladies came by and brought me some food and I had put my bed out on the screened porch to sleep in. As was his modus operandi, Dad didn't make it back the next day, but by early the following afternoon Dad, Mom, my two brothers and sister arrived in a car with a wooden two-wheel trailer behind it and Mom whipped up a warm supper.

When we first arrived, Dad preached at a church we were sharing with another denomination and like the church in Fabens, it had a swamp cooler. A swamp cooler was very much like a cooling tower at a power station. It was a box built with red wood slats were angled so that water cascaded down from the slats above and a large fan would blow the cooling air down into the sanctuary. Often if you were right under the down draft, you might receive a mist. The houses had no cooling and my choice of a screened in porch for sleeping quarters was defensive from the heat and during the rest of the summer, I was joined by my younger brother and sister with the baby sleeping with Mom and Dad.

I quickly began to investigate my domain. It became very evident that everything was spread out and I needed transportation. I found an old bike that I could get for just removing it from a junk pile. I had to put a chain on it and buy tires for the wheels which I bought with my wages from my first real job. I got to hanging around a slaughterhouse that slaughtered pigs from several pig farms in the area. I got real interested in the killing. The pigs were herded up a long wooden chute with a gate at the top. On the other side there was a tin chute with a steep decline. At the bottom was a gate that allowed the front legs and the head to poke out at the bottom. As they hit bottom, a well-placed 22 bullet ended their life. Immediately rope nooses were hooked on both front legs and the pig was hoisted up to a conveyor which stopped at stations along the way where the pig was processed and sent to the cool room for shipment to the butcher shops. I showed an interest in the killing and I received 35 cents an hour for killing on Monday mornings, Friday afternoons and Saturday mornings. I had funds to fix up my bike and see a Saturday afternoon matinee. I was flush with money and all was well with the world until my Dad let slip that I was killing pigs, not cleaning up around the place. I never told mom that I was cleaning up she just assumed that would be a job that they would give a kid. I had to quit and my chances of earning money were severally curtailed.

I really had a hard time understanding what my mom's objection was, but it was loud. After all when I was five years old, I was visiting her mother and dad and my grandmother asked me to go out and get the chicken that my grandfather had left on the back porch for our lunch. When I went out to get it, there was a chicken laying there with its legs tied up looking at me. You do remember my aversion for chickens. Those baleful eyes were looking straight through me. I went back in the house and told my grandmother that he left a live chicken with a head and feathers. I guess she just didn't think that a city boy did not know what to do with a chicken. She proceeded to teach me the art of killing. She had a steel hook that hung on the end of the clothesline and she slipped one end around the rope that held the legs and the other end around the clothesline. She then took a big knife, grabbed the head in one hand and cut it off with the other. As she cut the head she was quickly stepping back as the chicken would immediately begin flapping its wings as it pumped out its blood from the neck. Once the flapping stopped the chicken was taken into the house where she dropped it in a pot of hot water and we began to pull all of his feathers. The final thing was the belly was cut open and she reached in and pulled out the entrails saving the liver, heart and gizzard. From that time on when I was sent to the back porch to get the chicken, it arrived in the kitchen without a head. I really did not mind that at all it certainly got rid of my fear of chickens.

We hadn't been in Ft. Sumner for a month when one day my Dad arrived with a wiggling bundle of fur. She was a collie just like King and I named her Queen. Mom laid down the law right away. Queen was a dog and dogs lived outside. After mom would go to bed, I would let Queen in on the screened porch and she slept in bed with me. In the winter it was real easy to sneak her up to my room upstairs. She had plenty of love for the whole family and spent a lot of time during the day with my sister.

In the fall of 1951, I had a big brother (Mac) move into the house. He had been wounded in the Korean War and I really don't know the circumstances but through the Methodist Church volunteer families took in returning disabled Korean War vets who had no families. I remember him telling me about his first wound where he was shot south of Seoul by Chinese forces. His wound was in his belly and he was hit sideways opening it up where his intestines began to come out of the wound. He had to walk to an aid station where they were tucked in and he was sewed up and sent to a hospital in Japan. He was wounded a 2nd time this time he got a piece of shrapnel in his head and he was sent back to the states and discharged. Dad would take him to Walker Air Force Base in Roswell or Cannon Air Force Base in Clovis about once a month for a checkup.

I had a confident in Mac, I could discuss my cares and woes to a sympathetic ear and he taught me many skills a boy should know as well as an appreciation of Rock 'n' Roll specifically Bill Haley and his Comets as well as good Jazz.

My dad had to find ways to feed a large family and we immediately built a chicken pen and ordered chicks. We also, began to build rabbit hutches and Dad came home with does and bucks and we soon had kits. As the chickens grew up we butchered the roosters and as the kits grew up we butchered them. When butchered both were known as fryers. My mother, whose father was a farmer had no aversion to sending me out to cut off a chicken's head or club a fat rabbit by holding him by the ears and hitting him in the back of the head with a short club. Mac taught me a new way to kill chickens. He would grab two chickens by the head and start swing them around and then stop. The heads would still be in his hands and the chickens would be running around flapping with no heads. I finally understood the saying running around like a chicken with his head cut off. All of this was for the table. I never understood why I couldn't make money butchering pigs.

With my bicycle in operation, I soon learned that in the late summer I could head out to a farm where there was an apple orchard and I would get paid for picking baskets of apples. I soon teamed up with Herman who was and old frail Black man. I would climb up in the tree and drop the apples down to him and he would put them in the baskets. We would work on Saturday mornings and Sunday afternoons until the harvest was over. When we were in the field, we were the top pickers as I never was afraid of heights and he had big hands that never missed catching the apples. As the apple picking began to peter out, the cotton picking would begin, and we would team up again. He would pull one of the long cotton sacks and I had an old grain sack to fill up and dump into his bag. When the bag got too heavy, we would pull it to the trailer and it would be weighed and dumped and we would start over filling it again. We teamed up both falls that we were in Fort Sumner and I was not short of funds for a movie, popcorn, coke and a big Babe Ruth bar on Saturday afternoons as well as purchase my school clothes.

Early on, I made a pack with my mother to hold my money as my brother felt whatever was mine was his if he needed it. For the rest of my life at home, I could not keep funds at home. Either I gave them to my mom for safe keeping or I took them to a bank account that she had helped me set up and was a signer on the account.

As I mentioned, when we got there the congregation was sharing a church with another congregation. A short time after we arrived they began to build a church on the corner opposite from our home. Both the church and the house faced the main thoroughfare through town which was a highway on both ends. The church was being built out of bricks and when I got home from school, I would head over to watch the construction and see if I could find a job. I started out wheeling a wheel burrow with mortar. It was heavy for me and they let me start carrying a hod up the scaffolding to the brick layers. A hod is a v shaped box with an end on one end and a stick in the middle. You would carry mortar or bricks in the hod as it was not possible to wheel a wheel burrow on the scaffolding. So, I would join the men in carrying up loads. You would carry a hod by placing it on your shoulder (in my case a padded shoulder) and steadying it with the stick. In that manner you could carry about 4 bricks or a shovel load of mortar. You can imagine that we would look like ants moving up the scaffolding to where the brick layers were and back down to pick up another load. I was paid 2 cents a hod per level. My mother had kept an eye on me as she could watch from the house, but when we reached the fourth level on the scaffolding she pulled me from the job. That was devastating as in an hour I could earn as much as 80 cents.

By the end of spring the church was built with its beautiful stain glassed windows being put in last.

This was the best period of my relationship with my father. During the winter my sister and brother occupied two of the bedrooms and I had the big room in the attic to myself. I mentioned the grand fireplace down in the large living room. The first winter we were there that fireplace not only served as a cozy gathering place in the evenings when we popped popcorn over the fire, it was the only source of heat in the house. Of course, you know the designated person to see that there was a wood in the fireplace.

When I went to bed, I would have the fire going good and as heat rises I slept with a light cotton blanket in contrast to my siblings who slept with layers of blankets. When I woke up chilled it was time for me to go down and stoke the fire. I would have to stoke it as much as 5 times a night when it was especially chilly outside. By the second winter there had been installed a coal furnace in the basement. The coal would last much longer, and I seldom had to shovel coal into it more than two times. If Mac was awake which he was often with a head ache, he would have already stoked the furnace and I would not feel a temperature change and wake up. He had moved into my sister's room and she was bunking in my younger brother's room.

As I mentioned, this was the best period of my relationship with my father. I had a pump BB gun that was my constant companion, and I was a deadly sparrow hunter. My father would often go hunting with some of his parishioners or social club members. As I slept lightly, in order to stoke the fires, I was usually awake when he went off hunting. I decided to stow away in the car and go hunting with him. They were going duck hunting along the Pecos River and I was not discovered until we reached the destination. My father was not happy with me stowing away but from then on in, he would let me go hunting with them. I can particularly remember that we were rabbit hunting one time and I snuck up on a cotton tail rabbit who thought he was well camouflaged in some tall grass. Knowing that a deadly spot was right behind the ears, I got the muzzle close to the back of his head and let him have it. As I reached down to pick up the surely dead rabbit took off as soon as I touched him. I hadn't loaded the gun. From this time on until I was about 17 years old, I got to go deer hunting with my dad and they were very special times.

About 18 miles north of Fort Sumner was Alamogordo Lake (later named Sumner Lake in 1960). Like many lakes in the west, it was built by the Civilian Conservation Corps (CCC). The Alamogordo Lake was built on the Pecos. Also, about halfway to the lake there was a diversion dam on the river that expanded across two forks of the river and it was used to divert water into irrigation canals for the farms that surrounded Ft

Sumner. I had made friends with the school superintendent's son (whom I will call Jim) who was my age and he had a younger brother the same age as my brother. He had a bicycle and we often headed up to one of the dams to fish or hunt the abundant game around the lakes. It would take us about two hours to reach Alamogordo Lake with our fishing poles, BB guns, tackle boxes and bait and about half the time to get to the diversion dam. Jim and I had much in common in that because of our fathers we were supposed to be special. Jim got an allowance and all during our relationship he resented that I had more money to spend then he.

Fort Sumner had a wood lot where people disposed of old uwanted trees that had either fallen or were cut down and were not much good for firewood, such as cottonwoods. The cottonwood roots were porous and therefore one could cut one of the sizes of a cigar and mimic our fathers smoking a cigar. Jim and I had built a fort down on the wood lot with covering and all, where we could start a small fire and smoke cottonwood roots. Our little brothers not to be outdone did the same. We were sitting around our small fire puffing acrid smoke when we heard yelling. Our little brothers had caught their fort on fire. We ran over to help them put out the fire and when we looked back the wind had come up and our fort was on fire. The firemen worked all night putting out the fires on one square block of dead trees. Our fathers made us stand there at attention the whole time while it was being done. Of course, being the older brothers, we should have known better so we caught the entire wrath from our fathers. But our little brothers didn't come within arm's length of us for several months.

I was in the third and fourth grade in Ft Sumner and I had noticed that there were significant admired differences between boys and girls and that to tease a girl was the ultimate fun. I had a girl that sat in front of me in class. She was always so sweet to the teacher and she had long blond pigtails. Being a teacher pet was a death sentence to a boy in that time but it was totally expected of a girl. Also, pulling pigtails was a sure way to get attention from a girl. I often was making a head long rush out of our room with her hot on my trail.

One of my father's parishioners had a ranch on the Bosque Redondo and I accompanied my father out there on the occasion of a roundup. I learned how to ride a horse moving cattle and before I left there the rancher had given me a buckskin horse by the name of Tony to use for my very own. For the next year and a half, I would go out and saddle Tony up and help on the ranch if I could or ride to town to show off to my poor compatriots in town. On one of the occasions, I was riding on the south side of the canal toward a bridge, and we got there I jerked the reins to the right. The horse being somewhat of a cutting horse made an immediate right turn and I ended up with two big bumps on each side of my head. It took both me and Dad to persuade Mom that I should be able to keep on riding.

In the fall of 1952, I lost Mac. On one of their trips to Cannon Air Force Base for medical visits in the late summer, they drove over to Eastern New Mexico College in Portales, NM and Mac enrolled on the GI Bill. He came back for Christmas that year, but I never saw him after that.

My aunt, uncle and cousins were visiting on an occasion and the male cousin and I were on the road along the canal at the same bridge that I bounced twice on. My brother had gotten down on a ledge above the canal and my cousin was behind him trying to spot carp when I jumped down on the ledge and accidently bumped my cousin who bumped my brother who was bent overlooking into the water. My brother went headfirst into the canal. The water was moving along at a fast clip and he was bobbing up and down hollering when a man and his son, who was my age, went into operation. The man threw a rope around his son and he dove in and grabbed my brother who was already 100 yards down the canal. My father was so grateful that he bought the boy a brand-new Schwinn bicycle with a horn, lights and mirrors for saving my brother. I still had the bike that I had put together. It was the 4th of July 1952 when the Lions Club had a bicycle race and the top prize was a brand new Schwinn bicycle. I entered the race with my bicycle and was 10 yards in front when my chain broke and I was nosed out by the boy on the brand new Schwinn bicycle.

It was January 1953, when I received the ultimate present from my grandfather. It was a genuine Winchester single shot 22 long rifle and I began to supplement the rabbit hutches with cottontails. Jim and I spent many a day along the river shooting bullfrogs and hunting rattle snakes for their rattles.

My father's parents loomed large in our early lives and we spent a goodly amount of time at their home. While we were living in El Paso, we were only a few miles from their home and we saw them weekly. My grandfather was the general foreman at a large smelter, that accepted ore from all over the western United States and northern Mexico and on occasion I would get to go to the smelter with him. Early on my relationship with my grandfather was very deep. He liked to spend his evenings on the front porch with a cigar in his mouth and a little brown jug at his side with tequila in it. After a few sips and puff he would hand over the cigar and tip up the jug to my mouth.

My brother and I spent many a day building a fort behind their house to defend ourselves if the Indians attacked. There was a neighbor lady who was friend of my grandmother that lived a couple of blocks away. Her son whom was still living with her, was finishing college and he went on to be the head of a very large clothing manufacturer. I mention this because in one of her visits to the house where they only spoke German, she asked me if I liked horses. Are you kidding, I was the original buckaroo. She stated that she had a horse at her home that was lonely as the boys had all grown up and she wondered if I would spend some time with him. That horse and I became inseparable. We toured everywhere and whenever I got tired, I would signal for him to lie down and I would rest my head on his neck and go fast asleep.

As time went by, Grandfather retired but he still went to the smelter often, as he needed to spend time at the clinic there. My brother and I continued to spend a lot of summers with our grandparents while we lived in Fabens, but when we moved to Fort Sumner, our visits were a couple of weeks in the summer and every other Christmas as we alternated between grandparents for Christmas. I was paired with my youngest brother and my younger brother was paired with our sister for visits. Dad would deliver us and he always drove with his left arm resting on the open window of the car as he drove along with a cigar in his mouth. He was fair skinned and when we reached El Paso his left arm would be lobster red. (My father succumbed later on in life to melanoma, which started in his left arm.)

My visits with my littlest brother were great. Grandfather would arise early and I would be waiting for him. He would come into the kitchen and make up a batch of soda biscuits that were so light that if you didn't weight down the top of the pan, they would just float right out of there.

My grandmother would come in and start breakfast that would start with oatmeal and graduate to bacon and eggs to be accompanied with grandfather's biscuits and some of grandmother's pear preserves. On some occasions a potato pancake with be the third course, but always the fourth course was German Black Cake and a huge cup of strong coffee with loads of cream and several spoons full of sugar. Heaven help you if you could not eat it all, because the fateful words: "Vot da matter vit youse? Are you sick?" This could be the ruin of a whole day.

Often my grandfather would get his 41 Plymouth out of the garage and he with my youngest brother would head off to the clinic. It was extremely memorable to see my bald grandfather driving off with my bald brother standing beside him on the seat holding on to his shoulder and their heads were the same height.

I spent many a day with my grandfather working on the yard. We built low rock walls which partitioned off each side of the sidewalk and also on the property line. It was September 19, 1952 that rocking chair cigar and tequila sharing grandpa succumbed to the lung cancer that he kept going to the clinic for. It was the end of a very rewarding life that spanned being a cowboy, fiddler in the rotating dances of New Mexico, a policeman in El Paso and a conductor like his father on the railroad. I lost a treasure of stories of Old El Paso and southern New Mexico.

For all appearances, I showed up to church and lived up to all of the positive expectations of a preacher's kid in Fort Sumner, but life was about to change.

CHAPTER 4

W
e moved to Clovis, New Mexico May 1953. Dad and I hauled a load of boxes in the car and the little wooden trailer the 63 miles to Clovis. While we were there, we spotted a filling station that had trailers for rent with the name U-Haul on them and we left the little wooden trailer there and got a much bigger U-Haul trailer connected to our Nash Ambassador.

Trinity Methodist Church was just across the street from the parsonage and every time we pulled in people would be there to help us unload. Dad preached his first sermon there on May 17, 1953. The church was not like any other Methodist congregation we had ever encountered. The Church had always been the center of most of the social life of its congregation. It was built in the shape of the cross with the sanctuary in the foreground and teeing off the back of the sanctuary south side was the church office. Across the middle were classrooms and on the north end was as assembly hall, where social events occurred. The Rotary Club, Lions Club, Cub Scouts, Boy Scouts and Girl Scouts all met in the assembly hall just as occurred in other churches. But that is where it ended. The Methodist were always inclusive as opposed to exclusive in the dos and don'ts. Not this church. There will be no dancing. There will be no card playing. There will be no other music than what comes out of the hymnals.

The church was located on the west side of Clovis and was the smaller of two Methodist churches in Clovis. The Clovis Stock Yards were located less than two miles from our home and with an easterly breeze we got the full benefit of the sweet aromas emitting from it. I needed employment and all I had to do was follow my nose. I could not dream of a better job than moving cattle, sheep, horses and pigs through the pens as they were moved into the auction ring or loaded on trucks. I was a big kid and I had a job until the owners found out I was 10 years old.

My father suggested paper delivery and he went with me down to apply to deliver papers for the Clovis News Journal. I got a paper route just four blocks south of our home and Dad and I ran the route in the car, so I would know where to go. It was entirely in the segregated black section of Clovis. My job was being down to the back of the journal building at 4:00 AM in the morning to pick up my papers in canvas bags that I had mounted on the handlebars of my bicycle. I also had to collect for the papers on Saturdays by punching the cards that were sent to the customers with special punches for each week. To be successful I needed to sell more subscriptions, so I learned how to knock on doors and pitch the paper. There wasn't a more visible white person in that area than I was. Every Saturday, collection required a conversation about how things were going and I learned so many things from my extremely diversified clientele. I delivered a paper every day to a family that lived in a Cadillac. Man, that was one pretty car and there were four people living in it.

One of my most memorable clients was a very old retired merchant seaman. He had been all over the South Pacific and had obtained a collection of shrunken heads. I loved listening to his life stories.

Clovis was a dry county (no alcohol except for clubs) and a few miles to the east was Texas, which was dry all through most of the panhandle. In my delivery area was a rip roaring social club that was run by a big red haired Black woman (Sadie) who had rooms off of the club with entrepreneuring young ladies of the night. I couldn't collect for several subscriptions on Saturday as there was no money, and I was told to stop by when I delivered the Sunday papers and I would get paid. The Texans had made their visits and the place was flush on Sunday. The madam would say to me every time, "Now boy when you get a little bit older, I'll see to it that you get a bonus."

The route areas were fixed, and you could not deliver to residences outside your route, but there were no routes for businesses. There was a large restaurant two blocks from the publishing company called the Silver Grill where many farmers would gather early in the morning to eat breakfast and shoot the breeze. My dad and I went and talked to the owner, who was a member of the church and struck a deal, wherein I would leave 20 newspapers every morning and the Grill would sell them to whomever wanted one for a quarter and keep a nickel for their troubles. I began to solicit from other restaurants and before long I had bags hanging on the back of the bike for commercial deliveries. I did have a problem with the man in charge of distribution, but the publisher overruled him as the rules said protected routes were residential.

My paper route provided me with the money that gave me independence. The publishing company required that young deliveryman had to receive half their pay in government bonds, which were in $25.00 denominations. The rest of the money was for my use. I gave my mom money, and I went to every play, operetta and concert that hit town as well as bought my own school clothes. This bought me a unparalleled freedom to go and do things without having to obtain permission, but to only state where I would be.

The only traumatizing event I suffered in my newspaper duties is that I was headed to my delivery area with a full load when a young man passed me just as we were approaching an intersection at high speed. A cattle truck pulled out in front of us and he was going way to fast. He laid the motorcycle down and tried to skid under the trailer. The tires caught and the bike came up underneath and he was decapitated with his head flying and hitting my front tire.

I started the 5th grade at La Casita Grade School. La Casita was where most of the Hispanic children attended school and there was quite a few farm children from both west and south of town that attended it also. Clovis was not like any other town that I attended. King of the mountain was the order of the day and you had to fight for your very existence in a pecking order. I seldom went a day without getting into a fight as I was big for my age and it appeared that I needed to be put in my place. I really had no friends that could back me up as one block north of our home the kids went to an all white grade school and the young black men of whom I had made acquaintances with were all going to a segregated school.

Mr. Gatis was the principle and he had two well-worn paddles hanging on the wall in his office and I got familiar with the feel of them on my butt as well as the extra lashes I got from my father's belt when I got home.

Clovis was a very macho town and organized football started in the 5th grade. I joined the team, and we played the surrounding grade schools in Clovis, Portales and Texaco. It was full on tackle football. We had uniforms with pads and our helmets were made from leather. We learned to protect our heads and we never lowered them and hit someone with our helmet. Of course, there were occasions of bent noses. As the season went on, I got a reputation of a good football player and there was less demand on me to play king of the mountain.

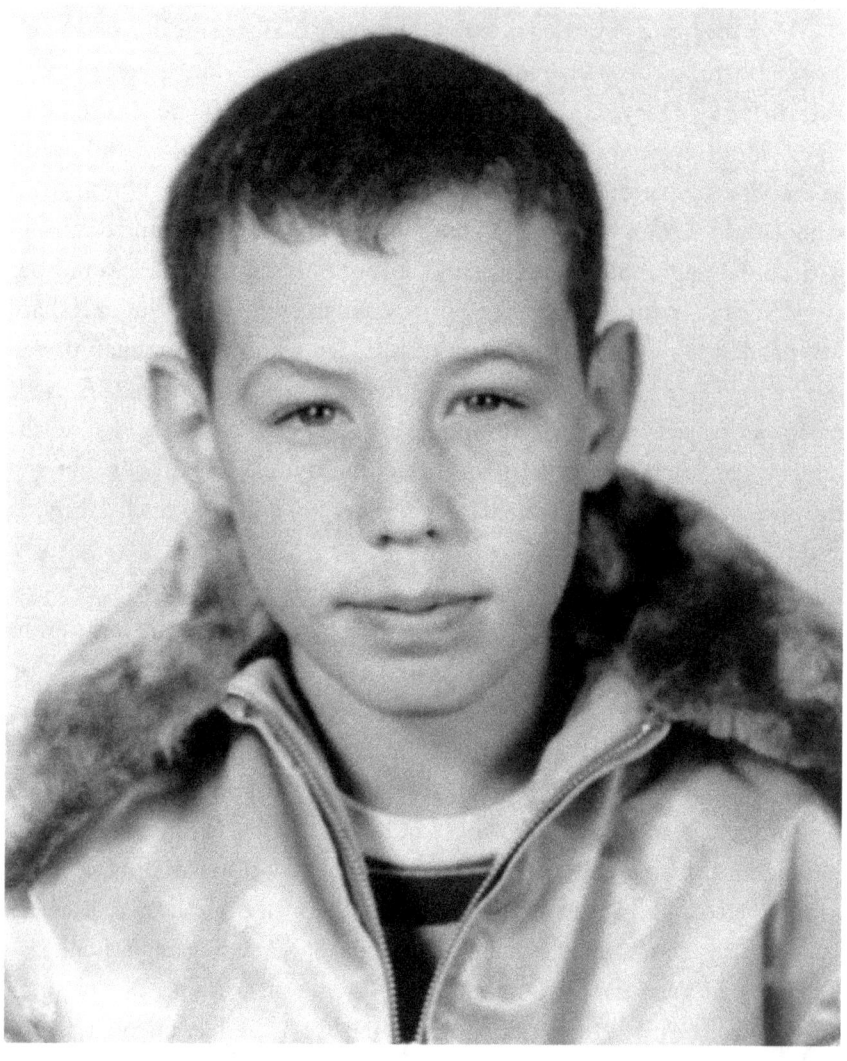

It was soon after the first of the year I was eleven years old and decided that I would like to play in the school band. After looking over all of the instruments, I picked the coronet as it was much manlier in sound as all brass was and it was not cumbersome to hold. My grandmother had begun purchasing war bonds in my name when I was born and they had reached their 10 year maturity and several of them bought my horn. I was soon relegated to practicing in the empty church at night as it seemed to bother my family at home. I will never forget how scary it was to go to that church by myself at night with the shadows of stately trees casting moonlit shadows that moved with the wind on the sidewalk. I really learned how to suck it up.

Brown vs. The Board of Education was decided by the Supreme Court that separate but equal was never equal and ordered the integration of schools on May 17, 1954. La Casita was integrated as it was the closest grade school to the adjoining area that the blacks lived in. All of a sudden there were kids as much as 18 years old in our six grade class. King of the mountain was no longer an issue and I did not regret not seeing Mr. Gatis

There were age limits and therefore there were no black students in our football program in 1954. As a point of machismo and how pervasive it was in the Black community. I had finished football practice and a black boy (George) that I had befriended early on in the neighborhood was going to go home with me. As we walked out of the school a farm boy accosted George and he was much larger than George. I took exception to his interference and we squared off. He was attempting to throw dirt in my face and kick me as I was landing punches. At that moment his parents drove up to pick him up and they began to cheer him on. He had tears running down his face and was swinging like a windmill when I landed a right cross to his jaw and it snapped. As we walked away his parents were yelling at me that I was a nigger lover and that they were going to sue my parents for the doctor bills. I got home with some scratches and my mother asked me if I had been fighting and I said, yes ma'am. She looked at me with her sweet way and said very pointedly in her southern bell accent. "Son, I don't want you fighting. I don't want you fighting at all, but if you do. You better never come home crying loser."

His parents did come to demand payment for medical bills and my father told them that they were theirs. They actually were cheering on the fight and were culpable in their son's injuries and there will be no funds forth coming.

George had an older sister who was 18 years old and she and another young woman got in a fight over a certain young man. These girls were not fighting like you see in the movies. They were squared off delivering blows as George and I were sitting on a low rock wall watching them. Of course, I knew George's sister and I began to cheer her on. Suddenly, the other girl turned toward me and hit me square in the mouth and said, "Shut your mouth white boy." I kept it shut as I got back on the wall.

I know that all of these stories sound as if there was an angel riding on my shoulder and that was not the case at all. I had a strong propensity to live on the wild side as one would say. It was Halloween 1954, when my neighbor (Woody) who was two years older than I and a couple of other boys got the wild idea that turning over outhouses would be fun as a prank. There were still outhouses in the neighborhood as many of the homes were built without bathrooms. Of course, when you turned one over and the owner came out cursing and yelling, that was real fun. The next morning there was nothing particularly said, as to who was to blame. Woody's dad and my dad knew their sons and we were put to work setting outhouses back on their slab or whatever structure supported them. Eventually we started getting help as fathers brought their sons over to the work crew.

On a small lot behind Woody's house was a building that housed a defunct laundromat. It was filled with hundreds of wooden cases of empty Nestle soda bottles. We could climb on the roof and remove a vent. It was too small to enter the building, but we could fish out bottles and ten bottles each would get us 40 cents apiece, which meant we were going to the movie and could buy a Coke, popcorn and a Babe Ruth bar.

I had mentioned the service clubs that used the church. The Rotary would have a breakfast meeting at 7:00 AM on Wednesdays and early on I would have to quickly get my papers delivered, as I had been volunteered by my father to help the breakfast cook prepare bacon, eggs and toast for the gathering. I learned to cook on the grill, which was very large and we would have an average of 60 Rotarians for breakfast. Of course, the first order of business was to get two large 30 cup coffee makers going and refill them both at least once during the meal. It doesn't take long to learn to crack eggs with both hands simultaneously and fill up a grill with eggs being cooked over easy, sunny side up and a solid yoke. That was after you had finished making stacks of buttered toast and bowls full of well-done bacon. There were occasions that the cook would be absent, and I was the cook.

On one of the Halloweens that fell on a Saturday night, the church had a party for the little kids where they played games and scared each other. The church employed a older black man as a janitor. He was to come in after the mothers and kids had gone home and clean the assembly hall and bathrooms. My friend Marvin and I had seen the comics of Stepin Fetchit and his ability to show wide eyed terror when he was scared, and we thought it would be funny to see it live. We donned on Halloween masks and waited in the broom closet for the janitor to open the door. We jumped out of the closet and he was gone so fast we had no way of letting him know it was us. We had to clean the hall and bathrooms that night.

By the time I was finishing the 6th grade, I had grown tall as high as I ever would at 5'11". I could all the rest of the earlier years of my life pass for older than I was. It was one summer evening when a carload of girls stopped at an intersection where I was standing and offered me a ride home. I accepted the ride and once we were in the car, they began to play with me and soon had my pants down. That was the first time I had gotten a female induced erection and it started me down a path of sexual experiences very early in life.

I graduated the sixth grade and was headed to a consolidated Junior high school where all of the grade schools sent their students for the 7th and 8th grade.

CHAPTER 5

I t was the summer of 1955, and there were three separate noteworthy events. The first was, I left my home on my bike, of which the brace that supported the fender had broken off some time before and I was somewhat used to it flapping. This time as I was standing and gaining speed the brace flapped right into the front wheel which came to a sudden stop throwing me head first on the pavement in front of the bike. When I got up, I had many scratches and lacerations chief among them was that my lower lip was impaled on the bottom front teeth. I walked into the house and confronted my mother with my mouth wide open and my teeth shining thru a mouth full of bottom lip. My mom got hold of the lip with two hands and pulled it off my teeth. She doctored me up and I went back to retrieve my bike and remove the front fender. As several spokes were broken, I had to find a wheel for it because I had to deliver papers the next morning.

My coronet playing was very much curtailed as I had no lip to fit to the mouthpiece for some time. It took me two years of practice to get back to the proficiency I had attained before the accident.

I had my first date. There was a blond girl (by the name of Kitty) that went to my church and I was in tune to the opposite sex. I asked her out to the movies, and she accepted. Come Saturday afternoon, I had gotten Dad to take me to pick her up at her house and he dropped us off at the movie. The movie was about ½ mile from her house, so we told Dad that we would walk home. When the movie was over with, we went to the soda fountain at the Rexall Drug Store where we wiled the way talking and having sundaes. It was finally time to head home as it would be dark

30

soon. When we reached the corner across from the Silver Grill, we parted ways as we each had a half mile walk to get home.

It wasn't very long after I arrived home that the phone rang and my mother answered it. She didn't say much other than offer her regrets and that she would talk to me about it. After she hung up, she said, "Tony, that was Kitty's father, and he is very upset that you let Kitty walk home alone." Of course, my defense was we agreed that we each had a half mile to walk and that there was no reason for me to walk to her house and then another ¾ miles home. My mother explained to me that when you pick a girl up at her home for a date, it is your responsibility to deliver her back home. Unfortunately, that was Kitty's and my only date. The final statement from her father was that I would never be allowed to date Kitty again. It would be several years before I ever dated a girl my age.

The Lions Club met every Thursday for breakfast, and it wasn't too long before I was enlisted by my father to be the cook's helper for their breakfast meetings. It was my duty to man the grill and turn out prolific amounts of eggs, bacon and pancakes to feed about 40 men while the cook deep fried potatoes, mixed batter etc:. I really got to hoping my dad did not feel that it would help his ministry to join any more service clubs.

It was becoming very evident that life was weighing in on my Mom. She had taken up smoking. She had to hide it from her family and heaven forbid the congregants would find out. The happy dare devil of my Mom that would go swimming with us had descended into a very introspective unhappy person. She no longer read to her children. She no longer told us stories that came from the inventions of her mind. She was a robot trying not to bring any gossip on her husband's career and she and my dad now slept in separate rooms. She smoked in the little storeroom off of the garage.

There was a new chain restaurant that moved into Clovis called The Spudnut Shop, which produced doughnuts from potato flower. There mainstay was the regular fried spudnut and its little brother (Spudies) a cake doughnut that was baked. Mom decided to go into business as The Spudnut Shop set up delivery franchises wherein Mom was called during the day for delivery of Spudnuts and Spudies and my little brother and I were called on to deliver the orders on our bikes with special canvas bags with hard bottoms that supplanted my paper bags in front and back.

We were required to wear the paper hats and a spudnut shirt while we delivered. Of course, there were extras in case someone wanted more or we were stopped in our deliveries. If any was left over, we would eat them. I finally got so sick of Spudies, to this day; I will not eat a cake doughnut. {Just an aside, it was 31 years later, after a meeting with people at the Federal Reserve Bank, I was driving a rental car to my motel in Sacramento, Ca. when I saw a Spudnut Shop and pulled in to pick up the most delicious doughnuts on this earth.}

Woody and I still had the cow shit cleaning concession on his father's cattle truck and we never had to use our earnings as we still had our bottle bank at the Laundromat.

Marvin's Dad ran a filling station and Marvin, who never was above making an easy buck had found out that a Mexican nickel (cinco centavos) was the same size and weight as was a quarter, which was the exact price of a pack of cigarettes. At the time the exchange rate was twelve pesos to the dollar and there were 20 cinco centavos to a peso. So when I visited my grandparents in El Paso and I stopped by Tony Lama's with my grandfather. I could sometimes get as many as 480 cinco centavo coins for two dollars. Marvin and some of the older boys were happy to shell out a dollar for 20 cinco centavo coins. It was about 5 years before cigarette machines got sophisticated enough to not accept cinco centavos for quarters.

When they built the nearly new junior high that accepted only 7th and 8th graders, they built a large auditorium that served as the culture place in Clovis. There were many traveling troupes and entertainers that would stop into our very classy theater to perform and I was always there decked out in a suit and tie. I don't believe I ever missed a performance. I tried out for performances put on by both the junior high and the high school, both who had open tryouts for performers that were of the school age or younger. I got parts in every one of the operettas, musicals and some of the dramas that I tried out for.

I also went to what was billed as premier movies in Clovis even though they may have been released a year earlier. Such was the movie Stalag 17, a movie that was a comedy-drama starring William Holden. It was the summer of 1954, when I got all decked out in my suit and headed for the movie house, as I had bought my ticket earlier to ensure that I had an orchestra seat dead center. As the movie progressed, I got very much into it. It came to a part where they were trying to get some information about some of the escaped prisoners and the Commandant had all of prisoners standing at attention on the parade grounds, when their pet puppy came out to stand with them. The Commandant ordered the Sargent (a large man who was kind of a bumpkin) to pick up the puppy and put him in a cloth sack and threatened to kill him. When the prisoners did not divulge the information the Commandant ordered the Sergeant to pull out his baton. Again, the prisoners would not talk, and the Sargent beat the puppy to death in the sack. At that precise moment a little boy jumped up in the middle of the orchestra seats and yelled "You Son of a Bitch". That brought the house down and I just sat there and hoped I would just disappear.

This was the era of the atomic bomb. During the school year we would have a fire drill where all the fire alarms would go off in the school and we would orderly march out to escape the fire. We also had atomic bomb drills and when the alarm went off, we were to get under our desk and kiss our ass goodbye. Of course, Hollywood found a very lucrative business in producing how ants, rats and other creatures got irradiated and turned into man eating menaces. My father loved horror movies and we never missed a one. It was 1952, when we saw the horror movie of all times. The 'Thing from Another World' grabbed you horrified you and scared you to death. As you sat in your seat you could feel the cold breath of death on the back of your neck. It was good.

My mom, whose father was a farmer and owned the local movie house had the opportunity to see every movie that hit town, on an occasion when she was home from college she saw 'Gone With the Wind', which was first released in 1940. Every four years it would be released again and make the round of the theaters. It was around 1952, when I got to go with my mother to see the movie. That movie stays within my memory ready to be brought up at any time. The scene at the Atlanta Train Station, that has been turned into a giant triage center and hospital, plus the fateful words "Frankly my darling, I don't give a damn" are always forefront in my mind. The fact that I got to see it several times with my mom was utterly fantastic.

The State of New Mexico made it illegal for grade schools and junior highs to have organized tackle football, so I was unable to play. But we did

33

play intramural soccer and in playing that I achieved what was called a second wind. It was amazing, you are about to collapse and all of a sudden you are running at your best and you felt like you could run forever.

It was the summer of 1955, when I had the opportunity of a lifetime. My father was to be a chaperone for a bunch of young Methodist College students on a trip to Philadelphia and I was going to get to go. There were two large station wagons and I sat in the far back of the one my father was in. Our trip took us through Tulsa, Oklahoma where we passed through a day behind a tornado. I never forgot the display of power that it left behind. Chief among these were straw sticking through electric poles. We camped out every night on the way and it was fascinating to be in the company of college kids. It was near the Fourth of July, and every town we went through some firecrackers were thrown out with yells that the South would rise again.

As we were passing through North Carolina, all the cars were stopped and the people were out looking at a young bear that had run across the road and scrambled up a tree. One enterprising photographer got right under the tree and took a picture with a flash bulb. The bear let out a yell and started scrambling down. It was a total riot as everyone was running toward their cars.

When we got to Philadelphia, we had reservations at a hotel. We were on the third floor and there were little balconies hanging on the side that you could go out on and look down at the world. One afternoon there was a thunder storm and lightning struck a transformer on a pole just across the street and below our balcony. That was one of the prettiest fireworks display that I ever experienced.

I was well aware of my propensity to sleepwalk and I was scared to death that I would walk out and fall over the iron rail on the balcony it made for some sleepless nights.

The boys had a day off from the convention and we headed out for Atlantic City, New Jersey in the late morning. There were no freeways at the time, and you drove through one small town after another. In one of the towns there was a movie theater that was showing a 3D movie, as none of us had ever seen one, we all went to the movie. It was absolutely fascinating wearing the glasses with the red and green lens and all of the caricatures and animals where right in front of our seat.

I had bought a Brownie camera for the trip so I could show my siblings the sights. I always carried it around my neck ready for action. While we were on the Boardwalk, we came upon a shooting gallery and I had to show off my skills at shooting the ducks and rabbit targets that were marching across in front of me. I won several prizes. I had set my camera on the counter and after I had pulled my Annie Oakley stunt, I set the gun down to find that my camera had disappeared.

When we left Philadelphia, our next stop was Washington DC. We toured the White House and the Capitol as well as the Lincoln and Washington Monuments. For me the piece de resistance was the Smithsonian. I could have taken up residence there.

Like most of the young men of West Texas and New Mexico we all wore western garb with fake pearl snaps in on our western cut shirts, boots and hats. I was walking with several of the college boys on sort of a river walk when we approached some young black boys who asked us if we were cowboys. The college boys played down their pretense but told them that I was a real cowboy. They went on to explain how I rode wild horses, tamed wolves and snapped the heads of rattlesnakes by grabbing them by the tail and snapping them in the air like a bull whip. They continued to tell them that I could whip any boy alive and I could outdraw Gene Autry. One of the young boys took off on his bike and shortly came back with a huge, big brother that wanted to see if I could whip him. I finally convinced him that it was not I that was spinning these lies and I knew he could whip me so there was no reason to prove it.

On the way home, we passed through a town and I was perched in my seat in the very back and everyone but my father who was driving was asleep with legs intertwined in all directions. I of course had to keep up the tradition and I lit a firecracker to throw out the window, which was closed. When it went off there was total bedlam in that car. It was a wonder that there were no broken legs or arms.

I have always been one to try it once anyway and I had been doing javelin and shotput for quite a while, when I decided to try high jumping and pole vaulting. I never was of the right kind of body build that should have been high jumping, but I had watched the Olympics in the news at the movies and I noticed that the Olympians were doing it quite different from the long-legged jumpers at school who were essentially high jumping like they were going over very high hurdles. Being short limbed, I found that I could best them by launching my body and fluidly clearing the bar backward leading with my head and arms and arching my back as I cleared it with my rising legs. The problem was those Olympians were doing the same thing, but they were attacking it from the side in the same manner and were coming down in a roll. I was coming down in a heap. On one of my descents my right knee got wrenched.

It was several weeks later that I happened to be walking toward my father who was walking home from the church, when the knee buckled as it was want to do and I fell down. My dad asked me about it and I told him that sometimes it just folds up all on its own and I fall down. He took me to a doctor that day who said that I needed to see a specialist and there was a very good one in Amarillo, Texas. Dad made some phone calls, and we were on our way the next day and that evening I was in an operating room. I can't really tell you what was done, but I do know it was about ligaments and it was further exasperated by my delay in issuing complaints. For the rest of my life I walked with a limp which was exasperated by lots of use. I spent six months in a cast that reached from my ankle to mid thigh and I had to use crutches to get about. Whether or not I would ever play in sports again was less than 50% probability.

My sweet grandmother who taught me the art of butchering chickens and always demanded sugar (a kiss) from me had mentally deteriorated and my Mom could not deal with it, so we just did not go to see her while she remained at home. When my Grandfather could no longer manage her dementia, she was brought to Clovis and put into some sort of a care home. She had been diagnosed with hardening of the arteries to the brain and she was at times very hostile. For some unknown reason she also became very strong. My daily routine was modified and I went to visit her every afternoon after school. As I was on crutches, a friend with a new Vespa motor scooter would give me a ride. I would walk in and the receptionist at the desk would call two attendants to take me back to her cell.

It was during this time, that I developed a healthy dislike for people that would build a fiefdom of power in their position and wield it with indiscriminate stupidity. Chief among those people were receptionists. For some reason the turnover was high and a new receptionist would look down at my grandmother's name and see "No Visitors" and never read the exceptions to the rules, which would cause consternation and delay until an attendant or the doctor on staff would point out that I was an exception to the rule. I really had and do have a hard time suffering fools. My grandmother was dangerous, but when I walked to the door she always uttered "Tony come here and give me some sugar" (give me a kiss).

It was right after lunch when I was at school, that two policemen came in and talked to the councelor who told me that my grandmother had broken away from whoever was attending her and broke down a door and was out on the sidewalk. The Home had called my other who informed them that my father (who could visit with her also) was out of town and they needed to get me at school to help as she was not capable. So, I was loaded in the back of a cruiser and we drove down past her as she was walking down the sidewalk toward downtown in a hospital gown. They let me out and they started to get out too, when I asked them to please not do that as they may agitate her. I walked to her on my crutches and the first thing she did was ask for some sugar. We walked to the Court House and rode up the elevator to the jail, where I walked into a cell with her. They shipped my Grandmother to the Insane Asylum in Wichita Falls, Texas.

It was December 17, 1955, when my mother delivered the only other child like me of six that had darker skin and dark curly hair. She was beautiful and I was totally enamored. Our whole family was ready for this baby as mom had suffered two miscarriages and each one of them tore us apart. Dad brought Mom home and we were all outside to greet our new sister. My youngest brother couldn't ply himself into a position to see Mom and the baby over us so he just climbed up in the elm tree next to road to get a bird's eye view. As he was leaning out, he fell out of the tree and broke his arm. Once Dad got Mom and the baby into the house he turned around and went back to the hospital with my brother who soon came home with a beautiful white cast. Of course, the first time I got a clearing, I walked up and signed his cast. He started wailing as if I had just beat him. His pretty white cast was marred. Mom had to explain to him that is the custom as she signed his cast as well as my other brother and sister.

The birth of my baby sister was a landmark for me. My mom who always told me I did not have to go to church, if I did not want too. Would answer my announcement that I was not going to church today with: "Oh, yes you are". As Mom sang in the choir, I had to go to Sunday school but during the rest of the Sunday festivities, I was at home taking care of the best little baby there ever was.

Christmas of 1955, I found a black Schwinn English Bike with brakes on the handle bars and three gears under the tree and it had my name on it. I had entered the modern age of transportation. It would still be several months before I would be out of my cast.

February 23, 1956, we got the news that my Grandmother had passed away insane asylum. I never again heard "Tony, give me some sugar." Being a preacher's kid, I had attended way more funerals than most people would in a lifetime, but this one stuck out on my memory for one thing. My Grandmother's sister who had also been a career schoolteacher stood by the open casket of my grandmother and as my sister, brother and I were ushered by she insisted that we give our grandmother a kiss.

It was the Spring of 1956, when I became aware of a dark curly haired girl that just pushed all my buttons. I had been in a play with her and she was a freshman in high school. Her father was a farmer, and she could throw a baseball harder than anybody I had ever known. Lorna was much wiser to the world than I but I was very much a willing student and we began to attend all of the functions in town as a couple. Leona was my first love.

In August of 1956, mother's sister and her two youngest children, who had been in Germany with my uncle where he was stationed supporting NATO forces, flew into Cannon air force base. They were to stay with us while my uncle and the two older cousins packed up and arranged to ship my uncles Porsche back to the states where he was going to be stationed in Albuquerque.

One of the first orders of business was for my Aunt to buy a car. It was a really nice day when my dad and aunt left to go look at some Chevrolets. Lorna had gotten her driver's license and she came by to pick me up in a car her parents had gotten her at the same time. As was my habit, I did not tell my parents where we were going but I did say we would be back early evening. We had planned a trip to Farwell Texas, which was a small town on the Texas side of the New Mexico Texas border. When I arrived home around 8: PM the household was in an uproar. My siblings were very distraught, and my mother and father were gone. My aunt explained to me that she had bought a new 1956 Chevrolet Bel Air and after they got home my dad took it out for a spin. He was headed out toward the Air Force Base at a high speed and pulled out to pass an old pickup just as the old man driving it started into a left turn. My dad T-boned him and when the dust cleared, he got out of the totaled car and walked up to the pickup where the old Hispanic man was not moving. He knocked on the door of a house and got them to call the police and tell them about the wreck and that an ambulance was needed. When Dad got back to the wreck the old man was out walking around cussing up a storm in Spanish. Just then the police and ambulance arrived and the moment they saw my dad they put him in the ambulance as his left arm was broke plum through at the forearm and was stair stepped. In addition, my father was not breathing well, armed with that information and the fact that he was asking for me got me speeding on my bike to the hospital.

When I arrived at the hospital, Mom ushered me into Dad's room where he was in a bed with a clear tent over it, as he had crushed a number of ribs and punctured a lung. I was standing right at the bed when he reached through and grabbed my arm and said, "Son I don't have anyone to conduct the sermon tomorrow. I want you to do it." He could have asked me to fly to the moon and I would do it and I could do nothing but agree to it. His arm retreated and the sound of escaping air diminished. My mom noticed the look of pure terror on my face, and she said, "Your Dad always types out his sermons, so all you need to do is basically read it. When I got home, Mom and my aunt had me read it repeatedly until it was second nature to me and that Sunday morning with my mother in the choir backing me up, I delivered the one and only sermon this ole boy was ever going to get close to.

I was pretty much a disturbance in my classes as was the case in grade school; I lost interest in the classes as they continued to repeat many of the things we had been presented with the year before. This got me in the councelor's office who had taken over that responsibility from the principal. I would get tested and I did know the lessons and was far beyond my class in everything but spelling. My mother's degree was in English education and she was very disappointed in my inability to spell and during my grade school years would grill me on spelling. Never the less the school Councelor recommended that I be put up as I was in danger of becoming intellectually lazy. My mother, who had been put up twice was adamantly against it for social reasons and the fact that I could not spell.

The junior high had plans for me. I only attended one class. I read my lessons in the councelor's office and took my tests there. As I had plenty of time on my hands, I became the councelor's assistant as she conducted testing throughout the school district, and I would accompany her and assist her on grading the tests. I was especially of good assistance for her in the schools surrounding the black portion of the city. My mother would not let me be put up, so they just taught me on the side and used my energies as an assistant. I just loved it.

All through the years, I have had a faithful companion that was always ready to give me some care and a nuzzle, whenever the cares of the world became heavy on me. In Fort Sumner, she graced my bed every night. We snuggled against the cold in the winter and slept with just a touch to signal I'm here in the summer. In Clovis, she roamed the allies with me pursuing any of the feline species that dared cross our path. We were the bane of all the tigers in our neighborhood.

On one occasion in Clovis, she was with me and my siblings in the front yard, when a man in a truck pulled up and grabbed her with a rope snare. As he was trying to put her in the truck, my siblings were fighting him. I ran in the house grabbed my Benjamin Pump BB Gun and put one well-placed BB in the side of his head. He released her and got in his truck as we retreated around the corner.

It was a short time later when I heard my mother call and we went to her. She said, "The police are here and you are going to have to go and talk to them. Your dad is with them." The policeman told me that they should arrest me for assault on a city official and he asked me why I felt I should shoot him. I explained that she would have never allowed someone to grab me like that and it was my duty to defend my Queen. After much confab, it was decided that I should not go off to jail. But Queen would have to as it was the law that she had to have a tag. My Dad and I followed the truck to the dog jail, and I bailed her out with a shiny tag on her collar for 10 bucks.

CHAPTER **6**

D ad had gone to the annual conference and it had been decided that we were going to head to Las Vegas, New Mexico. It was May 17, 1957 when we arrived at a parsonage that had three bedrooms on the ground floor which was about 4 foot higher than the ground. The bedrooms were portioned out to my mother (who was again pregnant), my father and littlest brother and two sisters. A stairwell led off a hall into a large basement that had a separate bath that became the domain of my brother and I. Attached to the brick house was a single garage that had a large storeroom on the back of it.

The church was somewhat a gothic style building with a large bell tower which had a walkway on the outside of the tower and a 4 foot high brick wall, that one could lean on and watch the goings on below. Behind the pulpit was seating for a large choir and behind them was a magnificent pipe organ with golden pipes reaching for the ceiling. The congregation sat in three sections of heavy wooden pews and covering the back was a large balcony with seating.

Underneath the sanctuary was a basement that had been partially developed into some Sunday school classrooms, but there was a large unusable space that was being used for storage and not much else.

The pipe organ was a steam organ and there was a boiler in the basement that fed the steam as well as a boiler for the steam radiators that lined the side of the sanctuary.

In the basement connected to the large room was a room that held the coal boiler that created the steam for the radiators, and it had a coal chute that led out to the street. The chute terminated in the basement in a storage bin that one could shovel coal out of and into the boiler. Also, next to the boiler for the radiators was the boiler for the pipe organ.

Mom was a farm girl that was raised in town and her father went out to work at one of his three farms. Animals were at the farm and were not allowed in the house. So, the first order of business was that I had to build a home for Queen in the back yard. I built her a large house with a pitched shingle roof. When I was done, I indicated to her that it was hers and she went in turned around a few times, came out and nuzzled me and went in and plopped down.

Employment was difficult to find, but you would have had to be a couch potato not to enjoy all the adventures that were afforded Davy Crockett, Daniel Boone, Huckleberry Finn and Tom Sawyer. There were farmers that had spring fed ponds where blue gill, large mouth bass and catfish waited for your hook as you drifted over them on a raft. Or you could lie in wait with your 22 for the muskrats that built their homes in the bank.

It was a short ride to the foothills of the Sangre de Cristo Mountains on your bike where you could hunt huge jackrabbits after the first freeze had ridden them of ticks. There was a mink farm that would pay you 50 cents per rabbit for them and you need not dress them out or skin them. Of course, Mom was happy to have some cottontail to fry up for a delicious meal and if it wasn't yet time to shoot rabbits there were prairie dogs that would whet the skills of the best of hunters.

Quail, pheasant and chukars had a habit of flushing under your feet and Mom would be very happy to prepare them for a meal if you were skillful enough to bring some home.

Premier for the intrepid outdoorsman was the pursuit of trout with a fly or if it was raining a bright spinner. Stream fishing was the only way for a real outdoorsman. One could cut his teeth on enticing stocked Rainbow trout with the flashing rainbow down their side. The excitement was even more when you caught a large German Brown Trout with red targets flashing on his side. But your skill was greatly tested after July, when you went high up into the Sangre de Cristos to match your skill with a Cutthroat trout that was spawned in the chilly waters of ice melt and had never seen the confines of a hatchery. Your fly needed to settle right in front of him while you remained hidden from the fish in the stream.

To catch your limits, you needed the supreme skill of a fly fisherman and the ability to patiently stalk your prey.

My brother and I had the great fortune to have been taken under the wing of Mr. Wilbanks who had spent his life fishing the streams of the Sangre de Cristo. He taught us how to hunt fish and the testament to his skill was he never had a bad fishing day. He would always limit out while we were beating the springs with our flys or changing to spinners or even heaven help us using bait. My father once mentioned in a sermon that Mr. Wilbanks could catch trout in the Sierra Desert.

We were headed up to one of our great streams that we had never seen another fisherman on. The La Junta fed into the Tres Rios High in the Sierras and it was open for fishing after July the 1st. There was a stream that flowed down a valley between to snow capped mountains and joined the La Junta as a rivulet no wider than a yard and about 8 foot deep that was concealed by poison oak. As one headed up the stream, it flattened out into a 2-foot-deep creek about 10 feet wide with many holes and boulders to shelter the wiliest of fish. As you traveled up the mountain, you would come up on beavers working on their dams that would scare the hell out of you when they slapped the water with their tail to warn their compatriots that and intruder was around. This is the home of the Cutthroat Trout.

I recall a wonderful story of how attuned to nature you are in a place like that. I remember Mr. Wilbanks had a new pole and reel, which would normally be sacrilegious. I asked him as to the reason why when he mentioned that he had been up on that stream working his way up and concentrating on the hunt when he heard a loud grunt. He looked up to see a big black bear, who had been working his way down stream fishing. They both were standing up staring at each other over about 8 foot of stream, when he said: "I just handed him my pole and all I could hear was the squeak of my waders as I headed down stream!"

My father, who was very ambitious to move to a large church in El Paso, not only for career advancement but to be nearer to my grandmother, sought to go about improving on the church by converting the large room in the basement into a recreation center as well as a meeting hall. To do this a large kitchen was planned and constructed. The Sunday school classrooms were rebuilt and the heating and lighting were modernized. My father fell short on the financing and pleas were sent out to my grandmother, who matched the congregation's contributions to the project at a very large cost to my father. She stated that never again should he come to her for money and she changed her will giving him a life estate into the income of the estate. The entirety of her estate was left to her natural grandchildren.

I found employment as a helper in the updating of the basement and was particularly fascinated with the laying of the shiny new asphalt/asbestos tiles on the floor. The floor just shined. There was a medium sized meeting room on one side with a meeting table and chairs as well as a television and couches. In the big hall there were two ping pong tables set up and I spent considerable time in the winter honing my skills of making a ping pong ball bounce erratically once it had cleared the net with a large amount of English applied. I won the state ionship in Albuquerque and my coach was my football coach.

I began football practice in early August and as all freshmen, I was assigned to the freshman team rather than the varsity. I weighed 185 pounds and could run the 100 in 10 seconds flat with or without a football uniform on. I preferred to play tailback as the coach was using a single wing formation, but my size demanded that I shore up the line and I was either playing as a pulling guard or a center. I lasted two weeks on the freshman team and I, as well as my friend Gene, were graduated to the varsity. Our team consisted of mostly Hispanic players as was the population of our school, which was one of three high schools in Las Vegas.

Although, one refers to Las Vegas as a community it is actually two communities divided by the Gallinas River into the communities of West Las Vegas and East Las Vegas. West Las Vegas was to my reckoning 100% Hispanic and East Las Vegas 60% Hispanic. Most of the positions on the football team were somewhat dictated by ethnicity. As most of the Hispanic boys were of slighter build then the gringo population and they were generally more physically mature than the gringo boys, they were populating the back field on both defense and offense.

The whole of the Las Vegas experience as far as socially was a nightmare. I had a complete immersive dose as to what it meant to be a minority. As far as the high school age kids go, gangs were premier and there were numerous gangs that radiated out of West Las Vegas and permeated both the Catholic High School and Las Vegas Robertson, where I attended school. In all practicality the gangs ruled life at school. The one place they could not touch was athletics at Robertson. They were in no way willing to submit themselves to a team or compete on individual achievement. They needed the gang to make themselves viable, because without them they were nothing.

It was September 27, 1957 when my baby sister was born. She was a little red bundle with peach fuzz for hair and she made our family complete.

Winter was an experience I had not ever had. When it began to snow, the ground in the shade never appeared until spring. There are many elderly people that live in East Las Vegas that were retired from the Santa Fe Railroad and I soon had hand snow plows and shovels with a circuit to make after each snow to clear their sidewalks. There was virtually no competition in the business. My younger brother, who was ostensibly a partner in the operation, was mostly not around to perform any of the work. I had a way to make money and it was very good on an hourly basis. If you got out early and worked all day to clear the sidewalks before there was any melt and freeze back, which you had to chip the ice off the sidewalks.

Although Queen had her own home, mother could not withstand the pleas to let her in the house when the back yard began to accumulate snow that never medlted till spring. Queen had plenty of love for six kids and would spread her time equally among us all. She would either be in the basement sleeping with me or up in the girl's room and my Dad was particularly favored with her company on cold winter nights.

Our mom started having mental issues soon after my baby sister was born and she did not participate much in the choir and was often in Albuquerque seeing doctors and staying at her sister's house. If it was during the school year she took our two year old sister with her. If it was the summer, she was left in the care of my ten-year-old sister. In between the times Mom was ill she attended Highland University and added another degree to her portfolio. The social conditions in Las Vegas were very hard on mom and she was at high tension until her children would arrive at home.

Mom slept in her own bedroom with my baby sister sleeping in a crib against the wall at the foot of her bed. As I had stated, the stairway to the basement originated off of my mother's bedroom and the door was open at night. My bed was just to the left of the stairway and I could hear whatever was going on in the bedroom. I have always been a very heavy sleeper going into a deep sleep the minute I shut my eyes but after about two hours I would begin to sleep much lighter. The baby would begin to cry and I was instantly awakened. It took no time for my mother to adapt to me coming up to see what was going on with the baby. I would check the diaper and clean her up and put a new diaper on if it was required and then I would lift her out and bring her over and place her on a breast and head for bed.

My little brother was a bed wetter, and my father would come down and get him out of bed around mid-night and take him to the bathroom. He would stand him in front of the commode and get him prepared and would give out a low whistle and my brother would stand there and urinate.

As I had mentioned before, my brother had been frail, and it was always my job to see after him and it was always my fate to receive the punishment meted out due to his miscreant and total selfish behavior. Later in life, I learned what narcissism was and the condition totally described my little brother. He was no longer frail, but he never carried his weight and I resented having to. Often when I would go up to take care of my baby sister, I would come down the stairs and walk over to the head of his bed and say ok and give out the low whistle my dad used. An instant fountain would arise and I would be sliding into my covers.

The tension between me and my father began to build. He would ask me if I would like to go hunting or fishing with him and we would agree that he had things to do and we would leave about 10:00 AM. I would prepare for our adventure, but he would never show. There was always a legitimate reason for not making it and it had to do with his occupation. I began to understand why the priests should never marry. After a while, I would no longer agree to go with him except when we were going with a parishioner, because he would never stand up a parishioner. It was amusing to both me and my mother that he considered us as part of his ministry and therefore our lives were pliant to the vagrancies of it.

In discussions with my mother, I would indicate that I did not want to go to church as I had seen some of the men, who set in their righteous pews and played their roles as sycophants on Sundays and during the week reverted to the debauched human beings, I knew they were. It was a parade of pretended righteousness and I hated pretention. My mother would say, "You don't have to go to church if you don't want to." I would reply, "Ok, I quit." And she would say, "No you don't."

It became my contribution to the ministry to keep the steam pressure up in the pipe organ boiler while all the singing went on prior to the sermon. I quickly learned that I could stoke the boiler and it would maintain pressure for the hymn after the sermon. I would then go sit in the balcony in a spot my father could not see me. It was easy to hear the theme of the sermon and be able to make some comment if it was required during Sunday lunch. After a while I just went to his office and scanned the sermon for reference. Once the sermon had started, I was off to the pool hall a block away to get in a righteous game of 8 ball and possibly collect someone's foolish bet. As I was sprinkled with coal dust, I did not have to be back to mingle with the parishioners after the service. During the winter I would have to hang around a little longer, to maintain the pressure in the steam boiler for the radiators.

I missed Lorna. Our relationship had been far beyond a movie and a soda and I ached for intimacy. For the first time, I actually had dates with girls that were my same age. We developed friendships, but they were basically charming companions and daughters of members of my father's congregation. All of our contacts were in the company of friends. Due to the dangers of the vagrancies of gangs most girl's parents preferred to deliver us to the movies and pick us up. It was on one of those occasions that my date and I along with two other couples were dropped off by the father of one of the girls, who was the publisher of the local paper. We got out of the movie before he got back and three pachucos came walking up to our group. One of them was carrying a 2 foot chain the other was beating his hand with a set of brass knuckles and the third had clipped razor blades on the end of his shoes. Two of us were linemen on the football team and were not there point of attack. Daniel was the only Hispanic in the group, and he was slight of build and suffered from Leukemia. We backed the girls up to the door of the theater and the Pachuco with the chain stood next to the ticket booth, which stuck out in the middle of two sets of doors to the theater. Pachucos live to dominate. They feed on fear and really do not want to begin a confrontation unless they are in the company of overwhelming odds in their favor. The boy with the brass knuckles kept saying let's settle this by going back in the alley so that we are not under all of these lights as he would punch Daniel. Of course, we were not going to be obliging, but it is a testament to their absolute belief in their dominance of the confrontation, they were not a bit wary that their aggression would cause them harm. On the third punch on Daniel, I was less than three feet from the chain wielder. I stepped inside and hit him with a low punch to the belly with my left and smashed his head against the ticket booth with my right breaking the glass. I had only seen it in the movies, but an unconscious person can just slide down a wall into a heap. I was immediately attacked by the other two and was fighting a backing up battle. The curb was rather high and there was a No Parking sign sitting right in front of the theater near the curb. As I was dodging the kicks and getting some punches in on brass knuckles, I stumbled backwards off the curb just as a haymaker was swung and a kick was being delivered at my legs. I just fell back and both the punch and the kick were terminated on the sign post injuring both of my assailants. They retreated when the girl's father drove up their companion laying there and calling us cowards, because we would not finish it in the alley. The father drove around to the alley and he counted 26 Pachucos in three cars.

My parents were not informed of the event. I am sure my father learned of it as the father that picked us up was a parishioner. But for my mother's sake it was never mentioned. It was less than two weeks later that my younger brother was knocked off his bicycle on his way home from school by a pachuco hitting him with a chain. Once he was on the ground, five of them surrounded him and started punching. The most egregious part of the whole incidence was there were bystanders including elderly men, who did nothing. No one even called the cops, because of fear of retribution.

During the winter months, Robertson High School would have a sock hop in the gym everyday during the lunch hour. The pachucos did not participate but they were there. The bathrooms were behind the bleachers and you had to walk down a long hall to the entrance. Both sides of that hall were lined with pachucos who would take punches at you. If any of the gringos needed to go to the bathroom, he would need to run that gauntlet. If I needed to go to the bathroom, they began to hold back, because I went through swinging with both arms. Also, they would stand other places and mostly be leaning against the wall. My little brother came over from the junior high school and we walked around, and he pointed out each of the five boys who attacked him, two of which were the chain wielder and the razor boy. As I walked up to them, they would be standing there with a smirk on their mouth and their head would be against the wall. It only took one punch each. They had never had a gringo retaliate and actually defy their gang. My little brother took off for his junior high and I was hauled into the principal's office. This was a unique circumstance for the principle as he had never had to deal with a gringo who was beating up on the pachucos and he had never had 5 boys be taken off to the hospital. My father was called in and the football coach attended the discussion as to what must be done. In the end, I was served some detention for fighting on campus and the football coach enrolled me in judo lessons so that I could learn to protect myself without needing to use debilitating force and have the skills to be prepared for the next round of retaliation. My father never heard from the parents of the pachucos.

One other note worthy event occurred along those lines. I had gone to the movies which were two blocks away from my home with one of my team members on the football team named Paul. Paul was about 6'4" and weighed around 220 lbs. As we were walking and walking up the hill toward my home, we passed the Optometrist Office where there were two cars parked in front. Just as we got between them the doors flew open and pachucos came out of them like clowns out of a Volkswagen at the circus and they surrounded us. In addition, there were two other cars on the other side of the road that emptied out also. They ignored Paul. I was their target. One of them grabbed my jacket and got right in my face yelling at me what they were about to do to me when I hit him with both fists at the same on each side of the head and yelled: "Run Paul!" I was very fast, but Paul beat me to the house. It is amazing what adrenalin will do. I ran into the house and grabbed the keys to my father's Buick and drove down the hill and up on the sidewalk trying to run over those that were still there. I tried twice to run over them and all of that time just down the street in full view was a cop car with a cop in it, who did nothing at all.

I took drivers training the first semester of the ninth grade. We actually drove a car and in our case, it was mostly in the snow. We negotiated the town streets and practiced driving around pylons as well as parallel parking out on a snowy runway at the airport. On January 23, 1958 I got my driver's license. It was Christmas 1957, when I drove the Buick down to El Paso to pick up my grandmother who spent Christmas with us. My Dad's rationale was I had finished driver's training and I was getting a license in January anyway. Man did I feel important.

I had struck up a relationship with a young man I will call Manny Marquez here. I was taken into the family very similar to my earlier relationship with Benny in Fabens. Manny's father had grown up in the Gallinas canyon near the Montezuma Castle which was a early 20th century winter resort built by the Santa Fe Railroad like a castle. In its resort years it was even visited by presidents. Down below the resort on the river were a series of ice ponds that the railroad would cut huge blocks of ice that were put in railroad cars lined with cork and filled with produce bound from California to markets in the East. As these ponds were no longer needed due to refrigeration, they became gathering places for people in the winter to ice skate. During the depression, Montezuma's Castle fell on hard times and at the time I was there was being used as a seminary for young Catholic priests from Mexico.

The residents of the canyon were of a religious sect called Penitentes which is a Brotherhood of Roman Catholic men. They practiced a brotherhood of penance rites that are secret and their High Holy Day is Good Friday. They guard those rites from the prying eyes of any but their sect and to do so they formed their own militia that no one would including law enforcement would mess with. An offshoot of that militia was the formation of the Montezuma gang which were the young men of the canyon who policed the safety of the canyon including the ice ponds and the seminary from the pachuco gangs. Manny was in that gang as well as his cousins. It was decided by that gang to offer me the protection of the gang as well as my family and siblings. I became a honorary member of the gang and it was broadcasted to the pachuco gangs that I was under the protection of the Montezuma gang. I always suspected that Monsignor Riefer (the head priest of the Catholic Church in Las Vegas) who lived at the priory of the large church one block away from our home and often had his legs under my mom's table for Sunday lunch had a hand in the persuasion along with Mr. Marquez. In any case I did owe fidelity to the Montezuma Gang.

My little 26 month old sister disappeared one day and when my mother became aware of it she totally lost it. She was just screaming and crying and we were all running around trying to find the baby girl when Monsignor Riefer showed up carrying her. She had wandered off and had walked into the Catholic Church. Monsignor Riefer stayed and consoled my mother for several hours until my father arrived and she went off to Albuquerque for shock treatment the next day.

In the spring of 1958, Mom hired a maid that was two years older than I; she was to help in the house. I am going to call her Rachel in this book. Rachel was a very comely Hispanic girl and I was immediately attracted to her.

I was riding my bike and just turned toward a driveway when the front wheel caught in a crack in the road and the bike twisted throwing me off against a curb where I hit it with my left shoulder shattering my collarbone with the left side of the break punched out of my skin. I was one block away from our doctor's office, so I went there rather than home. The doctor drove me to the hospital while his office called my parents. I was operated on that day and was kept in the hospital two days. I was sent home on the third day with my left arm in a sling which was bound to my body. It would be six weeks before the doctor would unbind me. A teenage boy can get awful ripe smelling when he is unable to wash under one of his armpits for 6 weeks.

I spent most of the six weeks of which I was banned from any exertion reading books and getting familiar with Rachel and our attraction grew. As the movie house was two blocks away, we went to the movies often where handholding morphed into heavy petting.

I would take Rachel out in my father's car and we began to have sex on a blanket in a mountain glade or the back seat of the car and even in my bed if there was no one around. We both were enjoying it and I know what love is. It was not love, it was desire and we both were hungry for the next climax.

CHAPTER 7

I t was the summer of 1958, and I had landed a job with a German farmer, who was also a conductor on the Santa Fe Railroad. The farm had two very long buildings that housed 2,000 laying hens. There were also some corrals with feeder calves and a very large barn that held hay.

My primary job was the irrigating of fields of alfalfa, grass hay as well as wheat and oats from a irrigation ditch that ran down the head of small 10 or 20 acre fields that were crammed into the small valley that the farm was fitted in. Our water came from Story Lake. There were no row crops and one irrigated by opening and closing gates in the lateral ditch after gates to the field were opened. Once the borders around the field had about two inches of standing water you would go down the lateral ditch to close the next gate and begin to open gates into the next field, then lift the closed lateral gate on the field just watered and quickly close the gates on the field just watered to keep the water from back flowing out of the field into the lateral.

I rode my bicycle out to the farm and I would leave home about 4:00 AM and be there when the water started coming down the ditch about 5:00 AM. Irrigation days were about 12 hours long and it was often 7:00 PM when I would arrive home. During the summer the irrigation days were two weeks apart and if you were not ready you just missed and lost production. My job also consisted of harvesting, a ten acre alfalfa field which was staggered so that one half of the field was cut and put away between irrigations.

There were two small Farmall tractors on the farm. I would hook a mowing machine that extended out to the right of the tractor tire and begin going in a circle mowing down the alfalfa. I would have 5 acres done early enough that I would be enlisted in running a small tractor cleaning out under the chicken pens and moving the chicken shit out to huge drying piles to later be used to fertilize the fields. The next day I would mow another 5 acres. If the first 5 acres had dried enough not to wad up when I raked it, I would hook up to a buck rake and form windrows.

When the windrows were dried, I would hook a flatbed trailer to the tractor and place them between two rows and with the tractor idling in first gear I would start pitching the hay on the trailer with a pitchfork. When the trailer was full, I would take it to the barn and put the hay where I was instructed to. If it was the loft, I would place it sideways to the doors and drop the hooks from above and swing it into the loft. If it was the ground floor, I had to back the trailer through the barn doors, which were exactly 4 inches wider than the trailer.

If it had rained, I would be enlisted in helping the owners'-brother-in-law who was deaf in maintenance on the buildings. We were painting a building and I was on a ladder and he was on the ground, when the ladder slid out from under me and I was hanging from a ledge. The ladder fell opposite from him and I had to drop a paint brush on him to get his attention.

My farming career ended when football practice started. I received a call from Manny; it was time that I backed up the Montezuma gang. I was to show up at third base on the baseball field at Robertson High with a baseball bat. I arrived and a group of guys saw me come in to the field and escorted me to third base. The gang had been challenged and there was a large group of pachucos in the stands hollering insults. We advanced in the stands and the pachucos started running out of the stands for the exits. I was given a ride home as it was quite possible that the pachucos would seek revenge for loss of face, on individuals walking alone from the baseball field. To my mother's inquiring look, I responded that I went to the baseball field to get in some batting practice, but there wasn't a pitcher and Manny and his cousin gave me a ride home.

It was two nights later, when we met a large group of pachucos at the bridge between the two towns and there was an all-out fight with chains and knives and bats. I was bare handed and found myself under the bridge in a fight with a knife wielder. My judo lessons came in handy and the pachuco was lying on the ground with the knife in his chest. I was totally scared that my life was over. Manny, told me no worries, the gang would take care of it. I did not miss a newspaper for several months and there was no mention of a body under the bridge or anyone missing. I came to believe the knife wound was not fatal and I was in the clear. I sure hope so. I was never in another gang fight.

CHAPTER 8

During my freshman year, I had lent $5.00 to a young man of whom his mother was my English Teacher. He decided that he really did not need to pay me back and if I forced him to, he would tell his mother that I was bullying him. I wrung the money out of him and received an F for the first semester of English. I transferred out of her class for the second semester. All I ever cared about was having a C average for the year and I did that without ever taking a book home or studying. My football coach and father had other ideas. I was going to be monitored and if I did not have good grades my sophomore year, I was out of football. I had made All North as a freshman and was looking forward to being All State this year, so I hit the books.

My sophomore year was unique in that I had a straight A average. I can't remember how we did as a team that year, but I as an individual made the All State team as a guard and center as well as a defensive end. The most memorable game was our game at Raton. We played that game and won it in below freezing weather with six inches of snow on the ground. The father of one of my team mates was a doctor and he was on the bench with us rubbing our hands to keep us from getting frost bit. His son was the only freshman besides me to play on the varsity the year before.

Rachel and I continued are liaison throughout the summer and fall without the benefit of contraceptives. It was the first of December, when my father met me at the door of our home and told me that I needed to go with him to the church. When we got to the Recreation Hall, Mom was seated on the couch and Rachel was on another with a man and women. I was informed that I was going to be a father. I was also informed that I was going to be the family to live and work on one of the ranches of the Fort Union Land and Cattle Company. I would be catching the bus every day to go to school and I would spend Christmas Eve and Christmas at home. I also was told when school was out, Rachel and I would most likely be moving to Grandmother's house in El Paso until the baby was born.

I was delivered to school the next day with my suitcases. I was to join Sara (the daughter of the foreman of the ranch) on a bus that would take us on a 45 minute ride to the main gate of the ranch. When we got there, a wagon drawn by four mules and piled high with alfalfa bales and sacks of cotton seed cake was waiting for us. Sara sat on the seat with her father, and I was perched on top of the bales with my suitcases. Sara's father was driving the mules and about 30 minutes into our ride he began to shout and whistle, and cattle would start coming from all over through a foot of snow to get fed on a well beaten feeding ground. It was my job to cut the wires on the bales and toss them over as well as empty cotton cake sacks as the wagon moved slowly over the feeding ground. We left there for another feeding ground about 30 minutes away and repeated the feeding of not only cattle but elk and deer that were comingling with the cattle.

About two hours after we had disembarked from the school bus, we would reach the house. There were two more wagons loading up 20 bales of hay and twenty sacks of cotton seed cake for the morning run and I stayed and helped get all the wagons ready for in the morning.

Sara had Cerebral Palsy and could walk haltingly with two crutches. She was a senior at Las Vegas Robertson and had been rewarded with a full scholarship to The University of New Mexico. One Saturday afternoon, Sara and I went riding out to a picnic area she knew a couple of miles from the house. It was February and the snow was patchy and mostly in the shade. It was just about time for us to head back, the horses inexplicably spooked and headed for home. We packed up our picnic basket and I loaded Sara on my shoulders (I doubt she weighed 75 pounds) and picked up the picnic basket. We had gone about a mile and a half when Sara spotted her father coming leading two horses from her perch up high. It was late February when my father came out and collected me to return home. I was informed that I was no longer going to be a father. My entreaties as to what happened were answered with complete silence. To this day, I do not know if I have another child out there or not.

Dad wanted to be posted in El Paso and I had no desire to live there. The doctor's son had applied and had been accepted to the New Mexico Military Institute. I knew that my parents could not afford to send me so I contacted them as to whether or not they might like to have an All-State Football player on their team with a 4.0 average over the past year. I received a letter back saying they thought they could scramble up a scholarship, but it would not be official until July 1st.

Dad struck out on El Paso and was posted to Deming, New Mexico. I was still committed to NMMI and I was helping to move the family to Deming. Mom, Kathy and the girls went down to Albuquerque while we boys packed up and moved the household to Deming.

CHAPTER 9

I t took me two days to land a job. I was to be measuring cotton fields for compliances on how many acres of cotton each farmer could plant. It was hot monotonous work, but my working companions were great. We started very early as to avoid much of the afternoon, heat. When I got home, I would shower and head to a drug store for a cold sundae at their soda fountain. Many years ago, I wrote about being captured by Deming and I am going to inject it here.

Deming Town

My family was moving from Las Vegas to Deming Town.
I had applied for the Military School and once my
family was settled, I would be moving over to Roswell.
This dusty little farming town wasn't for me.

I walked the streets of Deming to see what sites there could be.
Being a young man of 17, the sites I was hunting wore skirts
and had attractive smiles that made me happy to be alive.

It was near noon when I walked into a corner drug store on Gold, the
enchanting smiles of Diane greeted me. Things were already looking up.

That evening my restless feet took me to another drug
store on Gold, where I immediately spotted the winsome

Barbara and the alluring Mary Lou, who I found out were
varsity cheer leaders. I was beginning to feel alive.

Mary Lou invited me to a little party where she and all
the cheerleaders would be at her home tomorrow evening.
I was free, but I politely declined as I expected people
there would have dates and I would be alone.

Mary Lou called me that evening to tell me that her sister,
who was home from college, would like to pick me up and
escort me to the party. I accepted and began to wonder what
kind of fool would want to go to a school full of boys.

On the way to the party, sis mentioned that we needed to put in an
appearance at the party, and then she would really rather show me the town.
In all my travels from town to town, I had never been showed the town
like I was that night. Mary Lou would be my friend from then on. This
town was not for boys!

It was our first Sunday, and my father preached a particularly cheerful
sermon to the congregation and mentioned he had never been in a town that
had so many beautiful women and so many ugly boys. I resisted the urge to
give him an ovation. A beautiful woman came up to me an introduced herself
to me and said she was a farmer's daughter who lived out east of town. She
was curious as to whether I liked to ride horses. I told her that I loved horses
and had even had one at one time. She asked me out to the farm wherein we
would go horseback riding and swimming that afternoon. When I showed
up at the farm her parents were out visiting and I changed into a swimming
suit. There was only one horse so we rode double in our swimming suits with
her in back holding on to me. I was surely admiring this town. I worked
every day until 2 PM and by 4 the farmer's daughter would pick me up and
we enjoyed each other's company for a month until she mentioned that her
fiancé was coming to town and they would be getting married in two weeks.
We parted the best of friends. I still hadn't canceled my enrollment in the
Military Academy, but I really thought I was being a fool.

I had met Bobby at church, and he invited me to go with him to a
Farm Bureau Picnic. He explained that it was a big gathering, and I would

enjoy it. I participated in the races and contests, but my eye had strayed to a beautiful blond in pig tails, who was competing right along with us. I could see her smile and hear her tingling bell laughs as she determinately competed. I could no longer compete as all I wanted to do was watch her. As she got into a car with other kids to leave, I had no choice but to crowd in beside her. I was giddy with excitement as my heart pounded. I was not this town!

I continued to measure cotton acreage. A more mundane job you could not invent. It consisted of one person pulling a tape, which was referred to as a chain. Attached to his belt was a ring with 11 thick wire stakes hooked to it. As you pulled the chain you had one stake in your hand that was pulling the chain and when the fellow behind you reached the stake, he would give you a jerk and you would place the next stake. Both of you kept count at the end of the field, we would mark down how many chains and links the side of the field was.

Earlier in this book, I mentioned that I had a propensity to sleepwalk. One evening my parents had visitors from the church over and I walked through the living room in my underwear dragging a sheet and stopping often to place a stake. They did not wake me and I measured right on back to the bed.

We were measuring fields east of town in an area called Louis Flats. The field was next to the major east/west highway carrying traffic across the southern United States. It was about noon and we were headed away from the highway, when we heard a loud bang. We turned around just in time to see a Cadillac and Lincoln pointed straight up in the air and people were flying in all directions. We ran over to help and all of the passengers were black. There were twelve people in the cars, and we laid out on the highway eight very dead bodies. Ambulances arrived and transported the other four to the hospital only two walked out of the hospital.

These people were driving between Texas and California and they could only stop at motels that cater to Blacks. Unfortunately, those motels did not exist on that route and all they could do is fill up and keep on driving. Another lesson was learned on the inequities of the existence of our Black citizens that I first encountered in grade school with separate but equal. It was anything but equal. Even in Deming, the two Black families lived north of the tracks and the people of Mexican heritage did not mix socially with the whites. I had always been accepted in my friends' homes and I was not about to adhere to the mores of Deming society, which you will see in the future caused consternation.

We started football practice two weeks before school started. It was somewhat different from my Las Vegas experience. Our offense was the old T formation that was opposed to a single wing and sometimes double wing formations that I had experienced in Las Vegas. It was better suited to the players, which overall were much larger on the average than they were in Northern New Mexico. I was to play offensive tackle and defensive end. We had twice a day practices with the evening practice centered on conditioning. It was easy to see that we had a very good team.

During the late summer and school year, I settled into dating one of the popular cheerleaders. I never committed to her to be going steady, as I still had the pigtailed blond on my mind. She was going out with a popular rather pompous cowboy who was a senior, so I just stayed with the status quo.

As always, I participated in the church youth organizations and accepted offices I did not want. There was no pipe organ or amen corners in the church and as that I always had a job to go to after school when football season was over, I escaped some of the demands to further my father's ministry. I sought to be an example for my siblings and became celibate in relationships with girls of my own age. I had learned a hard lesson in Las Vegas and had no intention in repeating it. If I could not control the urges that had developed over the past four years, there was a legal house of ill repute in Silver City that I could visit. As time went by, distance, money and drive diminished the need to drive north.

We had a great season, and we were in the playoffs for the state title. We traveled to Farmington, where we were to play the first round toward the finals. Farmington played a double wing formation and most of their plays consisted of a fake to the middle with the tailback and the guards pulling out and leading the play left or right. Our defensive players had no knowledge of the play and our whole line would collapse inward to plug the line. The job of the defensive end was to turn the play into a line that no longer existed. If the end did his job well, the tackle and linebacker would interrupt the play and the end could join them in stopping the ball. I had learned my job well in Northern New Mexico, but the outside line backer was overwhelmed with two guards, a back and the quarterback running straight at him. Needless to say, it was a bad day at Red Rock.

We had two black boys, associated with our team. One was a half back and the other was our manager. They were teammates. The manager always had our uniforms ready. He was a model of efficiency with a smile. It is no wonder that he ended up with a string of laundries in one of our major western cities. We would not have achieved our run without our halfback. Unfortunately, he disappeared completely after our final season.

At the celebratory dance when we arrived home, our revered manager asked my date for a dance and she accepted. When they entered the floor, the organizer for the dance stooped the dance and said no Black boy would be allowed to dance with a White girl. My date and I immediately gathered our things and left the dance as did the entire football team.

The winter passed with me attending classes, dating the cheer leader, working out and working at a local grocery store. There was an announcement for try outs for a school production and I applied and was denied as I had already achieved well in football and therefore, I could not try out. The same thing happened in Las Vegas, when the band director said I had to choose between band and football. I rebelled against the school by never wearing the school letter. I was named to the all-state football team as a tackle and defensive end. I just did not know my place. There was no wrestling team to excel in and my trip to the state finals ended in Las Vegas. There was no baseball team, so my career as a center fielder and cleanup batter also ended in Las Vegas.

I had gone back to not studying or even bother to carry my books home in pretense. It was easy to maintain a C average or better in the college curriculum courses and I always aced the finals and the standard tests. I was sent to the office several times a year on suspicion of cheating. After all, one who does not do well on daily or weekly tests, could not possibly be acing the finals without cheating. My only achievement out of football was to bench press 350 pounds of weights 10 times at one exercise. Oh, I forgot that I did escort girls on the catwalk at the fashion show during the county fair.

In the spring, I was school a little early as I had a job at the local 7up bottler. A team mate of mine that was a year older had been working there for several years and he found me the job. I'm absolutely sure that candling the bottles as they came out of the machine for unwanted objects is the most mundane job and ranks up there with candling eggs in Las Vegas. I did like the job especially when we were not bottling.

Just before school was out, my cheerleader announced that she had been picked to go to Italy on an exchange program. I don't think I could have been more delighted. The pigtailed blond of my dreams was no longer affiliated with her cowboy, who had mistreated her and he had been dispatched by one of my friends and me and she was now free. I had tried many times to cool my relationship with the cheerleader, but as I had no where specific to go and her tearful entireties kept me in the fold I just remained.

Often during this past year, I had urges that had been satisfied since I was in junior high. There were frequent trips to Millie's, a legal house of ill repute in Silver City, New Mexico. Those trips ended later this summer. For the first time, I was in love.

I had landed a job temporarily on a ranch for $75/mo. and found. We worked a twelve-hour shift from 5 to 7 (add them up). It started with milking cows and ended with milking cows. To the consternation of the rancher, I would run 5 miles after work to stay in shape for football. During the late fall of the previous year, I had developed a case of ulcers and was on a baby food diet until I got to eat some white turkey meat. I was on a regular diet, but the rancher's wife was taking no chances and delivered me a glass of milk to wherever we were on the ranch for lunch. My pigtailed dream girl was up north on an exchange program.

After about six weeks on the ranch, my job ended and I went with my dad to church camp in the Sacramento Mountains. I had been attending the camp for a week every summer since we lived in Fabens. Needlessly to say, I knew the ends and outs of the place including the location of the girl scout camp a couple of ridges over. I developed a good income leading some older boys on a circuitous route in the dark to visit some lonely girls. I had also found the value of putting grass snakes in the bed of overzealous councelor's or people that had crossed me. This trip was much more mature and I talked my way into playing softball with a bunch of girls as long as I batted lefthanded (did not mention that I was somewhat ambidexterous except for throwing). I was in center field, when a girl hit a driving fly ball in my direction. I was not playing with a glove and like a true smart ass, of who was showing off, I reached up with obvious distain with my right hand to catch it. My wrist, of which I was not holding rigid, bent back stretching some ligaments. When I got back to Deming the doctor wanted to immobilize my wrist for a while by putting it in a cast. Having had casts before, I begged off and asked if I could get a leather cast that would allow me to take it off and bath. We had a local saddler and they built me a leather cast to the doctor's instructions.

The pigtailed girl was home and free and I wasted no time in asking her out. She accepted me and our date was set. I showed up at her front door and a very large man answered the door and looked down at me and said: "What the hell you want?" in a low rumbling voice. I informed him that I was here to pick up his daughter for a date of which he replied "The hell you say". I couldn't have moved my feet if I had wanted to, but I felt like judgment day had arrived. Just then a hint of a smile appeared on that great German face that I recognized from life with my grandfather, and he asked me in. My legs moved. We had a great time on our date and had sat down to pie and tea, when her brothers had tracked us down as she had overstayed her curfew and was in great trouble. Lucky for me, I did not know what went on, but she was grounded, and I had asked her out to a dance at the country club. With her mother's help, she waited until the night before the dance, to ask her dad if she could go and he relented. From that time on we were referred to as a pair and when we got our class rings in the early fall, I asked her to go steady and she accepted my ring. I was in dog's heaven.

My senior year in football, gave me a chance to play the position, I had played in grade school. I was now the full back and defensive end of the Deming Wildcats. It was the first game of the season and we were kicking an extra point when a little fat boy broke through the line and it was my job to stop him. Again, smart aleck distain raised its ugly head and I just got in front of him. My lack of all out effort got me on my back, and he left tracks on me as he went over me. I never again played a play of football that I played with anything but all I had. My goal was run over them or knock them out of the play, I was playing for keeps.

When I played a home game, my mother would always feed me a steak before the game. After warm up, before the game was to start, I would run over to the fence around the football field and my mother would come to the fence and we would touch hands before I went back to play. At the end of the game, the people in the stands would descend on the field to congratulate the team. The only one I saw was a girl with long blond hair that would fit under my right arm and escort me to the dressing room. A young man would show up also and ask permission to go with us. He occupied my left arm.

There was an old Greek man, who ran a saloon and restaurant. I always suspected that he also ran a book on games. Never-the-less I had a standing offer for steaks for me and my guests after the home games and we always took him up on it before we went to the victory dance. On occasion we would invite Jose, a team mate of mine, who was dating a blond girl that was the little sister of a friend of mine. When we arrived at the dance with that couple in tow, you could fill the chill, primarily from the chaperones. Nothing was said, as that was a sure way to end the dance if the football team left.

After the football season, I got a job with my dream girl's father, who ran a plumbing business. I was also back to being a lab tech for the science teacher. When finals came around, I aced them and ended up back in the principal's office, where they were trying to figure out how I had fooled the test monitors. It was during that time that my co-lab-tech, who was the brother of the little blond that went to the dances with us on occasion and I, were sent to the office. We were to take IQ tests. The test was a verbal test and you were to answer the question rapidly. Of course I began by repeating the question, giving myself a chance to mull over the various possibilities. After about five questions, the test giver stopped the test and said: "We are going to start over". He wanted me to say the answer that immediately came into my head. After the test, he said "I would like to help you join Mensa." He went on to say: "The IQ test was the Mensa test and your score was in the upper two percent, so you qualify to join." After his description of Mensa, I politely told him, "I am not a joiner, and I don't want anyone to know about this test". He replied, "The school ordered and paid for the test and they have a right to the results. But I can tell them about your desire for non-discloser. Why is it that you want this?" I replied, "They have all typed me as a football player and not allowed me to be anything else. So, I am just a football player. I know that the other person that took the test and my science teacher as well as previous councelors are aware that there is more to me than that, but it is a singular achievement and I'm proud of it. So, my organization will be the football team." It was shortly after that, when I got a letter saying I had been named to the High School All American team.

I had decided that I wanted to go to a university that had a wildlife program and the research that I did said, that Colorado State University had such a program. It was February, when one of my teammates and I departed Deming in my team mate's father's car with my father's credit card. We visited Adam's State University in Alamosa, Colorado, where my teammate was considering going and headed up to Fort Collins to CSU. At CSU, we were shown all of the facilities as well as the university. My high school coach had let them know we were coming. I was very new to the recruiting world. When I arrived back home my coach said, that I had offers coming in from the New Mexico schools as well as an Arizona school. He also said he had inquiries from Texas and California schools. I really did have a problem, I wanted my pigtailed girl to go with me, but I knew I was in no position to support us. My coach contacted CSU and told them my problem and that they would need to guarantee a scholarship for her as well as me with joint living quarters and meals. I did not tell her, because I did not want to start something I could not finish. My coach also let it be known to New Mexico State which was scheduled to start a wild life school the following year. New Mexico State was readily to make that offer and I was waiting on CSU. I had not taken my SAT as of yet.

I was really enjoying working with my pigtailed girl's father and brothers every afternoon and Saturdays and continued so throughout the year and into the summer. We would go hunting together and her mom would cook up our booty in great skillets and then bake it again with dripping gravy over quail, dove and rabbit.

I had attended mass at Santa Ana Catholic Church with my pig tailed girl several times when I told my father that I was going to Christmas Eve Mass and would help getting the Christmas presents put together when I got back.

Dad asked if I would mind if he went with us. Of course, I would not mind and my pigtailed girl was flanked my two Methodists who were not even closely versed as to when to rise, sit and kneel. We then went to the house, where my father went to bed and we assembled Santa's bikes and tricycles, before I took her home to Christmas kisses and a strong desire not to leave her.

My father attended a ecumenical group of church ministers wherein they decided that they would sponsor a ecumenical youth Sunrise Easter Service. My father quickly volunteered me to get it rolling by visiting all of the churches and their youth groups if there were any. My father should have asked me. I went about going to all of the churches and talking to their ministers about a Youth Easter Sunrise Service that would be held at the Spanish Stirrup Ranch where a chuck wagon breakfast would be served. The Ecumenical Council of Churches would be footing the bill. I would speak to the youth group if there was one with the permission of the pastors. If not, it was up to the pastors to get a count of who would attend. I have not named names in this story, but my faith in the institution of churches was forever changed by two visits two churches in Deming. The first was the Ruebush Church of Christ where I was told that as I was a non believer in the Church of Christ and I was to burn in hell. I knew members of the Ruebush family and I admired and liked them, but I would never again breach religious talk with them again. The second church was Saint Ana catholic Church or Saint Ann's, where I met with the priest. After I said my spill, the priest told me that no youth would attend a sunrise service from the true church. And if they did they risked excommunication. He then went on to get personal by telling me he was aware of my infatuation with my pigtailed girl, but that as far as the church is concerned it should end for her sake. If I was to marry her outside of the church, we would be living in sin. If I did not join the church, I would have to sign a document that any children will be raised in the church. He did not know that from that day on the word church became repugnant to me. I was not forsaking God, I was forsaking the man made church. I had never mentioned marriage to my pigtailed girl as I was still waiting on CSU. One night as we were sitting out in front of her house in the car she said, "You know if we were to have kids you would have to agree to them being raised in the catholic church. I did not answer, but the one thing I knew for sure was they would be the ones to decide if they wanted to be affiliated with a church.

My pigtailed girl and I had a wonderful spring. We attended the prom and afterwards we took off to the City of Rocks with another couple where we were to meet some of our classmates, who had gotten a bunch of Champagne with our contributions from Tillie in Palomas.

My father had a Buick Super 88 with 3 two barrel carburetors on the manifold. We had been driving it for about 5 years and it was a great car. The linkage for the accelerator was that if you barely pushed down on the gas only one carburetor would engage. If you stomped it, you could watch the gas gauge go down as the car screamed down the road. Just before the junior/senior prom my father thought he could do better if he just had one four-barrel carburetor and it was changed out. After the prom, we were joined by another couple and headed out to the City of Rocks between Deming and Silver City. We couldn't seem to find the party, so we shut the engine off to listen for the noise. We didn't hear a thing and decided there must have been a change of plans and we should head back to Deming. The car wouldn't start.

We were in a bad way and especially me as I had to be in Silver City the following day to take the SAT. I caught a ride with four Hispanic men to Hurly, and on the way they were talking about how pretty those girls were in Spanish. They dropped me off at a Circle K and I called my father about the car and told him about the men. I took off running down the highway and as I was running I started hearing a scream and a big cat was running on the apron beside me. I could not see him clearly as it was totally dark, but every-once-in-a-while he would let out a screech. I had run about 10 miles when a car came along and the driver was our assistant football coach. He saw the cat and said he was sure it had a long tail. When we got to the City of Rocks my father was there in another car and a wrecker was there to tow the car. By the time we got to Deming it was day light. My father and I had breakfast and I slept in the car back to Silver City.

Needless to say, I slept all the way to the test site. The test was a real challenge. The multiple choice portion of the test was no problem, but the parts that you read something and were tested on were very arduous as I found myself nodding off and the test is timed. I have no idea how I finished before time was up, but I did. I also did well enough that I would later be able to opt out on many of the low level freshman courses, which was not necessarily a boon for someone who had no experience in studying.

My Pig Tailed Girl and I had a good time as our senior year wound down. I still had not heard from CSU, but I had from UCLA and Texas.

New Mexico State was recruiting hard and I was beginning to think a lot about them as my girl was going there. I was working full time for her father and brothers and was enjoying it very much. It was in June, when my girl took my ring that was hanging around her neck and said she was giving it back to me, as we would be going to different schools and she wanted to date other guys. I told her I did not want the ring and she could do with it whatever she cared to. The next day I got hold of coach and told him to tell CSU that never mind the extra scholarship. I would be attending their school. I never told her what I had planned as she wanted to play the field and it was not going to work out for us. We continued to date off and on and even dated when I came home at Christmas and a small amount the following summer.

CHAPTER **10**

My father drove me to CSU in the late summer and he was very impressed with the school. The fields of flowers to be harvested and sent to flower shops all over the country were prolific and beautiful. I moved into the dorm and met my roommate who was from Chicago. I was the only freshman that was not matched with a teammate as a roommate.

The first day of practice, we were out warming up, when I was informed by the upper classmen that there was a initiation regimen that I had to go through. I informed them that I wouldn't do initiation. They informed me that I will. My retort was that I would fight every one of them, but I was not going to be initiated. I never was.

At that time, freshman played on the freshman team instead of the varsity. The coach told me that he was putting in an application for a waiver with the conference and most likely in a month I would be moved to the varsity. Shortly after that, I got a taste of college football. These guys were not interested in team. They were out for themselves and the existing varsity fullback considered me a threat to his position and instead of trying to beat me out, he began to try to injure me. The main problem was that I was bigger and faster than he was and when he was playing defense, I could make him miss with impunity and he became more and more hostile.

Both my mother and father were in Greek organizations and they wanted me to do the same. My first visit was to the one that most of the football team were members of. I was not impressed. My roommate wanted me to pledge his fraternity and I went with him. It was impressive. But they mentioned the initiation that went along with pledging. I told them that I don't do initiation and left. That was the end of my frat excursion. I still can' believe that I even considered it. I had always hated exclusionary organizations and these were the epitome of exclusion.

I was practicing with the freshman team until the waver came through. The coach was an idiot. He was a throwback to a time where it was thought that you toughed up players by having them run into each other. He created a gauntlet wherein there were two rows of players about 5 yards apart. On one end there was a player with a ball and on the other was a tackler. The object was the runner was to get by the tackler within the confines of the gauntlet. Of course, the only way was to run over the tackler. In my case the tackler came in low and hit me full force. I walked away limping. From then on, I could not plant my left leg and turn or push off on it without experiencing pain. We went down to play the freshman team at the Air Force Academy. I believe they had the whole freshman class of cadets suited up in football uniforms as there were several hundred cadets suited up sitting in the stands. I had learned early on when you had a new person in front of you whether he was on defense or offence you hit him as hard as you can. It tended to make them shy away from you. The problem was every four plays I had a new man in front of me. On defense, I was in the back field in every play, but when I planted my left foot, I had excruciating pain.

When we got back to school, the head coach had watched the film; He asked me what was wrong. I told him what happened, and the freshman coach had said, "You need to toughen up." The coach sent me to the infirmary where and ex-ray revealed a March fracture (The leg bone was fractured halfway through from front to back). My football was over for the year.

When an athlete goes to school on a full scholarship, his room, food, and tuition are paid for. What he does not have is money. He lives in a dorm or married housing and he and his spouse eat at the training table. The school will offer a job, which is usually at a minimum wage as not to run afoul of NCAA rules. The problem is if you are attending school, working out or playing and doing homework, you don't really get in many hours of work. If your family can't help out, the social life at college is extremely limited.

Colorado allowed alcoholic drinking at the age of 18, but it was limited to 3.2 beer. You could purchase a pitcher of beer for $1.00. The have-nots could gang up and buy several pitchers an outing and beer drinking became our social life.

As with all college freshman, what we take in courses is determined by our college entrance exams and our stated choice of what kind of a degree we wanted. My choice was wild life management. When I started my courses, it was heavy in botany. I inquired as to why a wild life degree was heavy in botany and was informed that there is no major in wild life management. Wild life management was a minor under a forestry degree. My whole life was turned upside down. The athletic department had misinformed me. I should have gone to New Mexico State. I was stuck in a school that was on a quarter system and I would not be able to change until the end of the year. I had no intention of telling CSU that I would not be back for a 2nd year.

The fact that I had no money, and I was totally disillusioned with the school let alone was so lonely for my pigtailed girl did not help me with the desire to keep my grades up. Another student and I started a fence building business for the many wealthy corporate executives that would buy small acreages and build a home and barn on them. We would put up white pole fences or wire fences to keep their obligatory stock confined in their property. After our first contract, we bought a small used Allis Chalmers Tractor with a post whole digger on the back and began to hire fellow students as we expanded our business. I did attend my classes and fought off the urge to sleep. I did not study on my free time. Needless to say, my grades suffered.

On the weekend I worked as a bouncer at a large 3.2 beer establishment. On Friday nights we had CSU students and on Saturday nights we had students from the University of Wyoming. I had to dress appropriately.

I never went to church while I was attending CSU.

I had one date that year in college. The girl that was my lab partner was a tall blond girl who hailed from a Montana ranch family and reminded me of my pig tailed girl. She went with me to the final dog races of the season. The number 1, 2 and 3 dogs plus some all-so-rans were featured in the last race. It started out with one of the fill in dogs on the number one pole. He made a good start out in front and the other dogs fell in behind him. He made the first turn and was still in the lead through the stretch. As he was coming out of the second turn he tripped and all the dogs that were right behind him crashed into him. The trailing dog that was coming off at 60 to 1 ran around the pile up and crossed the finish line. There must have been 10,000 people at the standing room only race and there was nothing but dead silence except for a few yahoos. I had not placed a bet.

CHAPTER **11**

I called my father and told him that I had a job on Oahu, Hawaii that included my transportation there and back. He said, "No the family needs you." I bought a 1941 Ford and drove home.

Between Colorado Springs and Walsenburg, I was flagged down by two comely co-eds from the University of Colorado standing by an MG convertible. One was headed for Trinidad and the other was headed for a ranch near Reserve, New Mexico. They loaded their baggage in the car and we headed south. I dropped the girl off in Trinidad and we headed south after her mother had fed us and given us some snacks and we filled up with gas. The car was a hard start, so I left it running when I filled up. I was never told to shut it off. By the time we reached Socorro, NM and filled up I had been up for 24 hours. We turned west toward Quemado and when I found a wide spot in the road I pulled over and slept for two hours until sunrise. At Quemado, we turned south and headed to Reserve. On the way south, we diverted so I could see Quemado Lake. That used up about 45 minutes. When we reached the ranch, the girl's father who had gotten a phone call when we left Trinidad was standing out in the front of the house demanding that we were over due for several hours and wanted to know what I did with his daughter. I wanted so much to hit him, but his wife and daughter were pleading with him and I suggested to him that he had no respect for his daughter and but for the women his pointed boots would be hanging out of his stupid ass and got in the car and headed for Deming. A good deed must be its own reward as it seldom comes from the postulating theories of a weak mind covered by a western hat.

It was 3 days before I landed a good job with Brown & Root Corporation which had a contract to build a cement portion of Interstate 10 extending east from Lordsburg, NM. The job was at the courtesy of one of the Hall brothers, who was the job foreman. I drove from Deming every morning in the 1941 Ford. My first jobs were driving a rolling compactor on the dirt of each side of the highway so that asphalt could be laid for the aprons on the side of the highway and to clear the hot asphalt out of the dump trucks that were feeding the asphalt laying machine. The temperature of the asphalt was between 275 and 300 degrees Fahrenheit when it began dumping and the temperature of the air was 100 plus. Needless to say I was drinking a ton of tea and my clothes were soaking wet. On the way home, I would buy a six pack of beer and have it drunk before I covered the 50 miles home. I also used a company pickup truck and a scraper to clean tar off the cement road. It was dripped on the road from filling the expansion cracks between the cement slabs. This was done between 10:00 PM and 6:00 AM, so that the tar would be cool enough to scrape. In addition, I was to watch the equipment left on the job. It was fun to watch some young men stop and run over to the equipment with a siphon hose and a gas can. They would get back to the car and pour it in their tank and take off with a great blue smoke screen behind them from burning diesel mixed with gas in their car. I flagged traffic on to the new highway while the detour was removed. Thus was my second experience with the racial inequities. As I was waving the flags and pointing in the direction, I could see a Black man in a big car staring down the road and headed right for me. I dove out of the way and threw my flags at him in the process. A flag broke his windshield and brought him out of the stupor before he ran into some heavy equipment. I was riding hook while we loaded equipment on trucks headed for Texas. Riding hook meant having one foot in a big hook and hanging on to the cable as the crane swung around to pick up a piece of equipment. I would hook the equipment up and ride it over to the trailer, where I would unhook and swing to the next.

I was offered the opportunity to go to Texas, which was really not my goal, it was also known that Halliburton was buying the company and the job certainty was unknown.

I moved back to Deming. I have been offered a job with the state of New Mexico it would not start for about one week. My mother had a washing machine, which had the tub mounted on a set of springs. Every once in a while, one of those springs would pop off if the tub was unbalanced. Mom asked me to fix it again. I was in the process of doing that when my father came in the door. He saw the washing machine with the top off and became enraged. This was his modus operandi when he got mad, he started hitting me. I grabbed both of his arms and pinned them behind his back and told him he that he will never hit me again. Mother all along has been trying to explain to him that I fixed the machine multiple times in the past.

It was a Sunday afternoon, and I had a date with my pigtailed girl. Her little brother came along with us. We went to a water pond on one of the farms and went swimming and I also shot bullfrogs. I cleaned the bullfrogs and took them home for my father who loved frog legs. He thanked me for the frog legs and told me that my presence there at the house was making my mother nervous and that I should move out. I left for Lordsburg the next morning.

There was a man and his son who lived in Lordsburg. His family were old members of the church. My father contacted him and he had a sleeping porch that I could sleep on. His son was about 10 years old and was anxious to play catch and be with somebody closer to his age. The arrangement worked well for about a week. One night I woke up with the man on top of me trying to kiss me. Needless to say, I was out of there. I moved into a small travel trailer in a trailer park that was owned by the county judge, where many of my co-workers were living. His home joined to the trailer park and he was always out watching us play baseball games or whatever we were doing in the evening after work. On one occasion, a football went awry and landed in the front yard of the house next door. I opened the gate in order to get the ball when I was attacked by a Chow dog that went straight for my neck. My left forearm came up under his jaws my right arm came around the back of his neck and his neck snapped. The owner came out screaming that they were going to sue me for the dog. The judge walked over and said you know you're going to sue him in my court and I saw that dog attacking him. I never did hear about any lawsuit.

This was a very dark time in my life. I never had another date with my pigtailed girl. The road we were working on was near Duncan Arizona. I was put to work running a transit level for setting grade stakes. The surveyor for the state of New Mexico was impressed in my abilities and gave me a book on surveying. I read the book during my time off in the evenings and the surveyor began to allow me to survey culverts. After a month of running the transit and level, he announced that we were going to Santa Fe so that I could take a test to be a surveyor. At the age of 19 years old I became youngest person to get a surveyor's license in New Mexico.

At the time that I was there, Lordsburg was a small town with four bars. I had been passing for 21 years of age since I was 17 years old and I began to drink heavily during the nights. The bars had ladies of the night and I began to sample the wares of the more attractive ones.

After about two months on the job on a Friday afternoon the superintendent of the job came to me and said the inspector had quit and I was going to be the new inspector for the state on this road. He gave me a book told me that Monday they were going to start pouring cement and I needed to know what to do to take samples and inspect culverts prior to pouring the cement. I read the book on pouring in covert construction, but I felt very overwhelmed. It was my job to check out the rebar construction and make sure that it was so many inches apart for each different section as per requirements. Once I was satisfied with the rebar, I would okay the bringing of cement. As per the instructions in the book I would place a core sampler between the rebar for each truck that came into pour. As the trucks were lined up to pour, I was say very pushed to complete my task. I had a helper who would remove the sampler and tag it with a tag that I gave him. It was up to the helper to keep the samples moist so that they would not cure too fast.

On road constructions there are many events happening at the same time and the inspector is responsible for the correctness of the job. This Inspector had several helpers working in different places at the same time, but it was his responsibility that things were done correctly. A helper may be setting up samples from compaction on the roadbed or checking the grades of the surveyors. It was up to the inspector that this was all going on at the same time and was being done correctly. Once the samples were taken and ready for transport they were sent to Santa Fe for tests. The inspector had no ability to monitor the test but in the end he was responsible for the validity of the test. As you could see, the inspector was set up to fail. My nightly visits to the bars and the comfort of a warm body increased over time as I could see this was not going to end well.

A portion of Interstate 10 was built over a playa between the Arizona border and Lordsburg. Within months after the construction, the road began to sink and potholes began to appear. Of course, the inspectors were the first people that were called up on the carpet. One night after several hours of drinking I went to the Blue Moon bar which was lit up like a Christmas tree. As I walked through the door a man with a microphone in his hand asked me what I thought about the construction of Interstate 10. My answer was loaded with expletives explaining to the interviewer what the role of an inspector was and his inability to affect the outcome of the tests. I was no longer the fair-haired boy of the New Mexico Hwy. Department.

My father had called the judge and told him that the Floyd Patterson vs Sonny Liston fight was going to be on TV in Silver City, and he wanted me to meet him at the Methodist parsonage to watch the fight. I got a push, and I was on my way to Silver city in the 1941 Ford. I parked in front of the parsonage and the Ford was on a downhill slope so I can get it started. I had no more walked in got a glass of tea and some cookies in my hand when the fight started. Fifteen minutes later I was back in the 41 Ford to Lordsburg. Liston knocked Patterson out in the first round.

Every two weeks I would head home for the weekend. The oldest of my sisters would wash my clothes and I paid her five dollars as it was very apparent she was be wore down with the responsibility of two little girls and the household.

New Mexico State had approached me again to play football for the school but I really did not have the heart to play football. I did contact a friend about going to school there. He was less than enthusiastic and told me the pigtailed girl had moved on and I would just be messing it up. I was offered a job by The Luna County Surveyor to survey a portion of the Gadsden Purchase that was in Luna County. Knowing that my time with the New Mexico Hwy. Dept. was limit, I accepted the job. I turned in my resignation and moved home.

I really enjoyed the job. We were retracing a survey job done 100 years before. In the original survey, they marked rocks with four dashes for section corners and one quarter for ¼ section corners. They then turned the rocks facedown so that they would not weather. This made the job very interesting as a lot of the places we were surveying were rocky hills. We ran many fruitless lines looking for marks on rocks. The wildlife we saw was utterly fantastic. On one occasion, we were going across a broad plain and saw a big black bush in front of us. As we got closer the bush it began to move, and it spread its wings. We drove under the bird whose wings were flapping on both sides of the truck. It was a South American condor. We saw a jaguar. We saw mountain lions and all kinds of wildlife. We came upon the ruins of the Mimbres Indians along the Mimbres River. There never was a day that we did not make a new discovery. Another time, my rod man was bent over with a white T-shirt on driving a stake, when I heard rush of air. I looked up to see a golden eagle diving on him. The eagle was after a rabbit. The rod man raised up just in time before the eagle would have struck him in the back.

Remember the interview at the Blue Moon Bar? It got aired on the Huntly/Brinkley report on NBC. My father and many of his parishioners saw it. Some of the parishioners were amazed and others had their suspicions confirmed. One thing for sure, I flunked preacher's kid.

The County Surveyor found out that I had drafting experience and my days of wandering over hills and dales were over with. I was now creating plats for the Deming Ranchettes. I was to create 1 acre lots and the access roads to them. Most of the lots would be in cul-de-sacs and I had to determine the degrees of arches so that the surveyors would have a plat to follow. In addition, the roads needed to drain in the natural direction that the land was drained. As this land was in the natural Mimbres floodplain, I had to find out what the high watermark was and design the roads to carry that water off. I was now a white shirt and tie employee.

My days were occupied with work. That evenings were occupied by going out with my buddies drinking. I got a wild hair and decided to ask one of the first girls I ever met in Deming on a date for Saturday night. Most of my friendships through my life have been with people older than I am. It was early Saturday afternoon when one of them drove up to my house and asked me to accompany him in a search for some guys that were peeking in on his daughter at home. We were riding around looking for just these guys when we were unlucky enough to find one. This particular friend name was Chacon upon seeing this young man he jumped out of his truck and started chasing him. I was sitting in this passenger side of his truck and it kept rolling right through a fence in up against a house. Chacon was still chasing the boy who was running into people's houses and running out the back door. While this was going on, I was having a difficult time explaining to the owner of the house that I was not driving the truck. By the time I got home it was 4:30 PM. My date was at six. I was really harried and by the time I was to pick up my date, my stomach was growling.

In this day and time $15 was plenty of money to have for a date. I had $25. We were going to a dance in Palomas, Mexico at a place called Tillies. When we got to Tillies. the cover charge was $10 a person. I only had five dollars left for the night. One of Tillies daughters was in our class in high school. I think she must've seen the exasperation on my face as she went and talked to her mother and her mother came over and told me that everything, I bought that night she would put on a tab. I could pay her later. Rather ironic that my first credit ever issued was in Paloma's Mexico.

I don't really know if we even had a good time. My stomach was railing I couldn't help but feel like I was passing gas and I was terribly embarrassed. The gist of this is that I never did ask that girl out again for date. It is rather ironic in this day and time that we are not hesitant to discuss bodily functions, but during that time it was totally taboo. That girl never knew that I enjoyed her company and I never asked her out on another date.

It was about 1 AM in the morning when the doorbell kept ringing. My family except for my younger brother was out of town and I was all alone in the house. When I got to the door, there was a young man standing there with a pencil thin mustache asking me where Gale was. I informed him that I had no idea who Gale was and to get the hell out of here. I slammed the door went back to bed.

It was November 23, 1962 when my brother asked me to go with him and a friend of mine exploring some mines. I don't exactly recall what kind of ore were in his mines, but whatever it was it was blacker than coal. I was black from head to toe. My companions wanted to stop in to one of the farms nearby where a girl was celebrating her birthday. There was no way I was going into somebody's house in my condition. I had been sitting in the car waiting for the guys to show up when a curly black-haired girl with a great smile came out carrying some chocolate cake. She said her name was Gale. Eventually my companions came out and I said goodbye to Gale, and we headed for Deming.

That evening my friend was still with me as we went out to do the Deming trot, which consisted from driving back and forth down the main street of town. We eventually met up with some friends and started drinking beer. I left my car at a empty lot and was running around with friends in another car. After a large consumption of beer, my friends began to tease me that the pigtailed girl was out on a date with whom we all referred to as the worm. This led up to one of the most regrettable moments of my life. We drove by the pigtailed girl's house and she was sitting out in the car with the worm. I walked over and tapped on the window. He rolled down the window and I just reached in slapped him and walked away. We were riding around drinking when some friends stopped us and said a cop was sitting by my car waiting for me to show up. Most of my friends were ready to take off for Juarez, Mexico. I was having nothing of that, and I asked them to drop me off at my car. My companion for the day went with me and I walked over to the police car. He rolled down the window and told us to get in. As I walked into the police station, I saw the worm and a friend of his standing near another policeman. He was crying. The policeman he was standing in front of was the police chief. The police chief told me that I had broken the worm's glasses and it would cost $50 to replace them. He then asked me if I was going to pay for the glasses. I said I would and he told the policeman that brought us in take us back to my car. On the way back, the policeman started laughing and said you scared the hell out of that wormy son-of-a-bitch.

My father was fully aware of what time we got in and at 5:00 AM he woke me up and told me to mow the lawns. It was still dark when I began to mow the lawn and my friend just parked himself up against a tree and carried on a conversation with me. He started harassing me about taking Gale out on a date. I really had no intentions of asking her out. Now you know my father was less then enthusiastically happy with me at the moment. I finally told my friend of whom I had found out was a cousin of Gale's that I would ask her out if my father would let me use his brand-new 1962 Chevy for a date. I had never asked my father for the use of his car. It was about 7:00 AM when my father came walking back from his office.

I told him that I like to go out on a date tonight and could I use his car. He said, "yes"! Being a man of my word, I called Gale up on the phone and asked her out for that evening. She said," yes".

We were dating at least every other night until she went off to college at The University of New Mexico. I soon followed her to Albuquerque and by February 28, 1963 we were living together. I had begun "The Loving of Da, Gail".

It was January 1963, as I was making my way to Albuquerque, when the news came that the federal government had cut off all highway funds to the state of New Mexico until they had cleaned their house.

CHAPTER **12**

I t was March 2011, when Gale, her cousin Mattie and I attended my 50th class reunion. We were sitting at a large table much of my high school football friends and their spouses. There was a large screen in the background that was showing a picture of me and my pigtailed girl as Mr. and Miss Deming High School. One of the wives of my football friends went over to a table to talk to the people at the table and I saw it was my pigtailed girl. I went over and asked the young lady if she would introduce me to this lovely woman. Jeanie Marie Schultz Ford immediately jumped up and moved into my arms. That haunted me for several days before I could put it on the back burner and go on with life. After a short conversation, Jeanie went over and talked to Gale and Gale brought her up on our life. I sat down and became acquainted with Wayne Ford, Jeanie's husband.

I lost Gale on February 17, 2012. We had a celebration of life in early August 2012, when everybody could attend. I sat and stood at the door and greeted every person that came in the door. There were over 300 people that attended her celebration of life.

It was April 2012, when my youngest brother and I made a trip through the Panhandle of Texas. We were examining the lands that we had oil rights on. To our chagrin there was a producing oil well on one of the properties.

It was March 2014, when I completed the book "Loving Da Gail". I threw myself into my business. I still had over 50 properties that I was managing and I did make a few sales.

It was fall 2014 when Macho, my Rottweiler, and I took off on a bucket-list trip. We went to Albuquerque for a few days and then headed north on an adventure. We stopped at the Pecos Indian runs, which I had not visited since I was in high school. We visited Fort Union in New Mexico and Bent's Fort in southern Colorado. We then headed for St. Louis where I wanted to do some family research for both the book and family history. Macho and I thoroughly enjoyed St. Louis. While we were in St. Louis, we took excursions to find gravesites of early relatives. We left St. Louis and headed for South Dakota and Mount Rushmore. Macho and I thoroughly enjoyed Mount Rushmore.

We left Mount Rushmore for southern Montana. In a small town, we parked our fifth wheel in an RV Park and the next morning we headed toward little Big Horn. What a fascinating place it was. Every place a soldier died at is marked. It is a very expansive battlefield.

The next day we began our trip toward home. We drove west to Montana and then south to the north entrance to Yellowstone National Park. Macho was fascinated with the geysers, buffalo and moose that we encountered. With the fifth-wheel we could stop at anything that fancied our imagination. We left Yellowstone and headed south to Jackson Hole Wyoming. The elk were already gathering in the preserve and Macho was out of his mind with excitement.

We continue to head south and when we got into Utah, we went over to Wabash Range and headed down the east flank of the Wabash range with the eventual goal of landing in Eager, Arizona. Along the way we stopped and looked at anything that fancied our attention. We visited with my grandson and his family before we headed to Tucson.

It was January 2016, when I sent a letter to Jeanie Ford asking her to allow me to escort her to our 55th class reunion. I knew Jeanie had lost Wayne the year before. She was out of town when the mail was delivered. It was about a week, before my phone rang and Jeanie was on the other end. She accepted my invitation and we talked about our lives. This was the beginning of nightly phone calls between two lonely friends.

In February 2016, Jeanie informed me that was she was going to visit her daughter in Albuquerque. I arranged to visit my sisters in Albuquerque at the same time. I went over to Jeanie's daughter's house the first evening I was in Albuquerque. I had asked her to go out to dinner with me. Just as

I arrived, Jeanie's daughter and her husband arrived. We were talking in the driveway of their home. I felt the presence behind me, but I continued to talk for a short time before I turned around and lost my breath as Jeanie was standing there. I visited her daughter's house several times over the next three days before I left for Tucson.

Unfortunately, the week before the reunion my bladder stopped up. I had to have surgery to have a catheter put in. The only way I could attend the reunion was with the catheter. I was not going to wait for another year and went with the catheter. I removed the catheter the day after I got home.

Two weeks after the reunion, I got a letter from Jeanie that stated our relationship was too soon after she had lost Wayne. I wished her good life, continued on writing a book that I had titled "Ranchero" and managing properties.

It was May 1, in the evening, when I began to have unbearable pains. It felt like I had been penetrated with a spear and my chest and back were hurting intensely. I drove myself to the hospital and when I arrived, they immediately put me in a room to be examined. It turned out that I had blood clots in my left lung. A couple of days after I had been stable, they did an echo on my legs looking for blood clots. They found them in my left leg. They were traveling up through my heart into my lungs. I already had lung damage. I had five stents in the larger arteries around my heart and the blood clots passed through them. Without stents, I would have been dead before I ever left for the hospital.

After two weeks I was sent to a nursing home. They showed me the cot that I was going to sleep on the sheets were soiled. The place was filthy, and the inhabitants looked very sad. I told the people at the nursing home that I was leaving. My family took me home. Twenty-four hours later, I was back in the hospital and after a week I, was discharged to home.

It was a month later, when I went in to have an operation on the opening to my bladder. During the operation, biopsies were taken and they came back cancerous. I had more biopsies taken on the external part of my prostate and they came back 75% cancerous. Within weeks, I had begun a series 47 sessions of directed radiation therapy.

It was the end of August when my son, Martin, accompanied Macho and I on another bucket-list trip. This was to take us up through the Dakotas into Canada and across Canada to Niagara Falls. Our goal was to visit great fishing and the cities of Canada. We were then going to enter the state of Maine and play tourists headed south and west. I wrote a travelogue on this trip so I'm not going to recite all the locations that we went to or what we did other than when we entered Canada, they would not allow Martin to go any further and we had to turn around and follow the Great Lakes on the southern end until we got to Maine. We visited friends along the way and had a great time. I had some health issues that had to be addressed but they were not bad enough to keep us from continuing our adventures. This trip lasted about eight weeks.

When we arrived home, and I had the time I began to gather up the travelogue and edit it before I sent it out to my readers. I sent Jeanie a copy and she called me on the phone. It was early January, and I had decided with a friend to stay at his home in Las Cruces around the 15th of the month. I also decided with the librarian at New Mexico State University to do some historical research and I told her about the topics that I would be researching. In our phone conversation, I mentioned to Jeanie that I was writing a new book and if she was interested, I would like her to proofread what I had written. She was interested and I planned to visit her the day after my trip to the library at New Mexico State. I also was going to get copies of documents from the county recorder in El Paso.

As it turned out, when I arrived at the library, the librarian had said she had sent a note to me telling me she could not find anything on the subject that I was doing research on. Unfortunately, the note was sent the day I left for Las Cruces. I left and I had plenty of time so I went on to El Paso and the county recorder's office to get some documents. I totally struck out. I headed back to Las Cruces to my friend's house and I left there the next midmorning for Jeanie's house.

We had a great visit. I had sent Jeanie a copy of "Loving Da Gail" as well as parts of "Ranchero" which would become "Estância Del Pérez". We began our nightly phone calls and I visited her a few times before we met in Albuquerque. We had a family gathering and my family reacquainted with Jeanie and met her Albuquerque daughter and family.

It it was May, when we gathered in Tucson for my friends and family to meet Jeanie. My youngest daughter and her family flew in from Los Angeles later that evening evening so they missed the party at my home. The next day we got to meet them for lunch and afternoon at a resort.

It was Christmas Eve 1965, when I last went to a church service. I had been to funerals and weddings in churches, but I had not attended a regular church service. I had not given up on God. I had given up on man's church. This was easily done within my marriage as Gale was an Agnostic.

It was January 2017, when I accompanied Jeanie to her church. I was extremely apprehensive but the small congregation was accepting and somewhat curious. One of the congregants had known of my father and my youngest brother. I was highly impressed with the preacher, who stood at the head of the aisle and delivered his sermon. It was the third or fourth time I attended church that during the sermon the preacher said, "Only through the church could one find lasting salvation." As always, Jeanie and I were holding hands during the sermon. She felt the shiver that went through my body. I could not accept the church was the sole arbitrator of my relationship with God. I apprehensively continued to accompany her to church. I loved to sing the old hymns of my youth and the preacher delivered some great sermons. My father would be very happy.

Jeanie and I have spent the last 4 ½ years in a very loving long-distance relationship.

La Vida Seguira